CREATIVE CHRISTIAN EDUCATION

CREATIVE CHRISTIAN EDUCATION

Teaching the Bible through the Church Year

HOWARD HANCHEY

MOREHOUSE-BARLOW
Wilton, Conn.

Morehouse Barlow Co., Inc.
78 Danbury Road
Wilton, Connecticut 06897

ISBN 0–8192–1380–2

Library of Congress Catalog Card Number 85–63571

Printed in the United States of America

10   9   8   7   6   5   4   3   2   1

To

ANNE, STEPHANIE and ASHLEY

and

a Host of Others

With them all, I learned Sunday school is fun.

Contents

Contents

Preface

Every year there is a big turnover in Sunday-school teaching personnel, so things are always a little bit changed.

For the rest of us, however, almost everything is completely new.

The first part of this book paints a bright picture of what good Sunday-morning Christian education is like and what it can accomplish. The second part describes proven educational plans.

Particularly in the early chapters, important points are highlighted with phrases like THE FACT IS, POINT, and THE BOTTOM LINE. They are designed to get your attention and help you organize your thoughts as you read.

I want this book to *work* for you; it has been designed and written as a manual, a tool.

I also want to explode several myths, namely that

1) Christian education is something that happens *only in the classroom*;

2) Christian education requires a *professional* teacher and a group of *willing* kids; and

3) Christian education is primarily the transfer of factual *information* about the Bible and teachings of the Church.

We need another view, the central premise of this book: Teaching is not primarily *our* ministry; though we teach, it is primarily *God's* ministry, a ministry to us, taking place in the classroom, in Sunday's worship, at home, and in the marketplace. And its result is faith's birth and growth.

What you won't find in the following pages is a way to organize *some* of your parish for Christian education, because this is a book about organizing the *whole* parish. I mean everyone and everything, and for this reason: God has stories to tell. To name only a few:

—the story of God's relationship with Israel (All Saints, Epiphany, Lent, and Easter/Pentecost);

—the story of your parish's ministry (the Epiphany term);

—stories of Paul's discovery of Jesus (the Epiphany and Easter/Pentecost terms); as well as

—stories told on bulletin boards and in chancel dramas (all terms);

—stories of the Good Shepherd (the Epiphany and Easter/Pentecost terms); and

—stories of folks like you and me, helping God take care of his world in our daily work (the All-Saints term).

And more; when everyone celebrates these stories week after week, an educational symphony of gigantic proportions develops. The whole parish sings.

By the time you finish this book, you will have in hand some clear options for organizing your Sunday-school year, and you'll be equipped to decide what will work best in your "shop."

"So," you wonder, "where do we begin?" First, put this book into someone's hands and charge him or her to begin. Get a "spark-plug" person with whom people like to work, someone they can trust. Second, expect him or her to share this book with many others. Then watch a vision take shape.

Next, you will probably see people appointed to:

—organize a parish registration campaign (chapter 7),

—publicize the dream, first in the parish and later in the local community (chapters 2 and 3),

—develop teaching teams (chapter 7),

—decide on Sunday curricula materials—whether "store-bought" or parish-generated (chapters 3, 5, and 8 to 13), and

—figure out the logistics for term-ending festivals (chapters 3, 6, and 8).

You will also, in all likelihood, see the nine-month school year divided into six-week segments and the whole parish focus on one theme. Specific content may differ from class to class, taking into account pupils' ages and interests, but the central theme will hold everything together. Baptism, for instance, might be the focus for Epiphany, but the various classes may handle it in diverse ways.

All the while you will be watching a parish celebration develop— because this kind of Christian education is like a big parade.

I owe some thanks to a lot of people.

Balmer Kelly, professor emeritus of biblical theology, and Neely McCarter, formerly professor of Christian education, and both former deans of Union Theological Seminary in Virginia, helped set me free to value my own curiosity and imagination in scriptural study. Ross Mackenzie, once professor of Church history there and now again a parish priest, also encouraged me. At my seminary, the Reverend Dr. Frank VanDevelder, professor of Old Testament, has occasionally provided me with the sort of patient assistance that makes his teaching great.

I am also a clinician, and a lot of what I know best I have learned while helping others.

I am a Sunday-school teacher and a parish priest, too, and now I teach in the seminary.

I have worked as a hospital chaplain, and on more than a few occasions I've stood by the bedside of the dying. I have suffered with others late at night in hospital emergency rooms—tough theological questions are asked then, though they never go by that name—and I regularly counsel people trying to get their lives together or to sustain a marriage.

This book draws on all that experience. But most of all it puts together what I have learned by working with a lot of good folks who have happily consented to join me in the Sunday-morning Christian education endeavor. They're not named here, and I regret that, but nonetheless their contributions fill this book.

What you are about to read is not theory (though when we first began our work, we wondered what would succeed); it is a distillation of first-hand experience. All of it has been tested, and all of it works.

The Virginia Theological Seminary H.H.
Alexandria, VA
January, 1986

PART I

A Vision for Christian Education

CHAPTER ONE

To See Visions and Dream Dreams

A SUNDAY-SCHOOL TEACHER SPEAKS

"I don't think anyone knows what goes on here!" Peggy Barton snapped with anger. I listened closely, for she was a conscientious Sunday-school teacher.

Her story unfolded, and what Peggy Barton described seemed to be true.

To be sure, we had plenty of books and the funds to buy a wealth of other materials tailored for pupils of every age. Peggy, however, missed an overview fitting the classroom task of Christian education into a comprehensible whole. The Sunday-school classroom was isolated from worship, and though written curricula materials were abundant, there was little coordination among clergy, teaching personnel, and parents. To Peggy everything was fragmentary; there were many pieces but no picture. She felt alone and helpless.

A BOOK IN TWO PARTS

This is a book about vision. It is divided into two parts.

The first part, chapters 1 through 7, details why and how a good Sunday school works and what we can expect of God's interested participation in it. Illustrations abound.

Chapters 8 through 13 constitute the second part, which puts into practice what part one described.

Both parts detail a practical vision that has been proven to work.

VISION IS THE KEY

It is easy to get lost when we have no map to follow; it is sad when we get lost though we have the God-given elements of a map already in hand.

When God's gifts are used in concert, parish Christian education can sound like a symphony; when used separately, as they often are, parish Christian education sounds more like noise, which is what Peggy heard.

I have been involved in parish Christian education since childhood. I have been a pupil, a teacher, a parent, and I've served as assistant and associate to the rector and as rector of a church. I can't remember a time when the life of a Sunday school was not important to me.

Ordained leadership, however, has shaped my thinking most, and it is what separates this book from most Christian-education manuals. Most other manuals center on the art of teaching in the classroom. They provide a lot of bright and lively material, but they cannot discuss the Sunday school from the perspective of parish administration, for the authors have seldom had primary responsibility for week-to-week parish leadership. They have never had to struggle with how Sunday-morning Christian education fits in with everything else, like parish calling and hospital visitation, Sunday-morning worship, the Every Member Canvass, and so on.

I shall address the bright possibilities of teaching, too, but I'll refer to the greater issues as well.

The following chapters detail what I have learned. All my suggestions work; they have been proved in practice. Anything that has not worked you won't find here.

YOU CAN BE CREATIVE

You may be one of several thousand neophytes assuming a role in this year's Sunday school.

Why so many, one wonders? One great hymn puts it thus: "Time like an ever rolling stream bears all [of us] away."[1] Life is always moving one generation into its predecessor's place, and God is always making things new. As a group, we Christian educators are always a little bit old, but mostly new.

Best of all, we have on hand a magnificent collection of materials;

all provided by God, for the most part they are already in place in parish life, and they're free. Here is a list:

— Scripture,
  — the Church's history,
    — clergy leadership and support,
      — the interest of persons like you, responding to God's call,
        — Sunday's worship, and
          — the experiences of pupils in the classroom.

Each component is readily available, awaiting our use.

Imagination is the birthplace of creativity. This book will have accomplished its task if it can excite your imagination. It is designed to help you catch a vision of what a Sunday school is like when it is really working well.

THINKING THINGS THROUGH PAYS OFF

How to put these several components together, that is the question . . . and, all too often, the problem.

In the following pages you won't find an exact solution for every problem, though some solutions are there. Rather, I offer an opportunity for your mind's eye to catch the vision of what these materials look like when they function together smoothly.

I hope, as you read through this book, you shall form a vision that will be a reference point from which you can make carefully considered decisions about what is important in your church and your classroom. Ultimately your dreams and visions are best; they are triggered by imagination and curiosity, and God uses them to develop in us hope and confidence.

A CHRONIC PROBLEM: LACK OF CLERGY INTEREST

Just ask, and many clergy will aver that they are ill-prepared to take an active part in the organization of a Sunday school. No one likes to feel inadequate.

Rarely, in most seminaries (looking across denominational lines), is Christian education considered a central ministry of the Church. Of course there are exceptions, like the Center for the Ministry of Teaching at the Episcopal Theological Seminary in Virginia, but generally Christian-education course work is elective at best. At worst it is neither valued nor offered. Even when the subject is not neglected, it is taught more as cold theory than as vital opportunity, simply because students are not actively involved in planning and teaching.

This bleak picture gets bleaker still. Most clergy, on graduation from seminary, are yoked to a senior pastor who delegates responsibility for the parish's Christian-education program to the new assistant. It is a job the senior minister has grown out of—often thankfully. This attitude is an albatross around the parish's neck; certainly it hangs heavy on the shoulders of the staff. It is a yoke neither light nor joyful.

The new assistant—with little preparation for the task, even less vision of the possible, and a lot of apprehension—begins work. What little enthusiasm he or she has may soon be dashed in the harsh discovery that parish Christian education not only takes time but seems fundamentally impossible.

Given this background, it is not surprising that Christian education takes a back seat in parish ministry. It seems to consume too much (already precious) time, and there seems to be little rhythm and no rhyme or reason to it.

As a consequence, too many clergy simply give up and refuse to participate. It is a wonder we do as well as we do.

THE POINT: If enthusiastic clergy leadership is missing, it is difficult for the hopes and aspirations of the parish laity to be realized. This is nowhere more evident than in the enterprise of parish Christian education.

Vision empowers leadership. This book offers shape to the vision and details the tools that can help implement it.

A CONTINUING ASSET: PARENTAL INTEREST AND SUPPORT

Parental interest is also important. Happily, we do not have to twist arms to engage parents' able support for Sunday-school Christian education; by and large the parents are already keenly interested.

Researchers have found that Christian education is the major reason most young families come back to Church. But it is not education for themselves in which the parents are most interested; it is in an educational program for their children.

These parents are not about to leave their children with a stranger in some carelessly arranged room; they look for careful planning, organization, and responsible care.

When Sunday school is exciting and children beg to go back, it "is a factor in people's decision to plug into a church." My own studies confirm the report of the Alban Institute.[2]

A study (attributed to *Time* magazine) describes the importance of parental interest and the way it shapes that of the children.

> The survey notes that if both parents attend church with their children, 77% of their children will remain faithful in church attendance as adults.
>
> If only the father attends church with his children, 55% of those children will attend as adults.
>
> And if only the mother attends church with her children, 25% of those children will attend as adults. And if neither parent attends church with their children, only 6% will be faithful church attenders as adults.[3]

I have for several years conducted a similar straw poll of my students, and the above statistics have proven startlingly accurate.

Also, parents remember the Church as a "belonging place" from an earlier time in their lives. Most speak of the importance of a "warm and friendly congregation," reports the Alban Institute.[4]

But what of those parents who say they must leave a decision about Sunday school and matters of faith to their children? They are saying much more about their lack of interest than about the freedom they want for their children. I've also found it is not helpful or productive to argue about it.

My children, for instance, do not have a choice about whose surname they bear; my wife and I made that decision for them when we married. When our children are older, they may choose to redefine their heritage, but they will never *not* be of their parents' flesh and blood, always sharing our hopes and expectations.

The Christian Church is a special kind of family. At its best, it is a place to celebrate God's presence in everyday life, to hear again of God's mighty acts in the past, and to be encouraged to look with eyes of faith for his gracious hand at work in the world today.

My children had no choice about their involvement in the Christian community. Like their parents, they are in it for the sake of saving knowledge. Later they may choose to turn from it, but it will be a turning away from something their parents think important, not something denied them because of their future freedom of choice. Just as they are Hancheys because my wife and I are of that name, so they are Christians because we too are of that faith.

Parents play an important part in forming their children's attitudes. Our children learn from us by what we say and what we do. So enlisting parental interest and support for any Sunday-school program is crucial. With it, great things can happen; without it, Sunday school is reduced to a child-care service.

THE BOTTOM LINE IS: The best way to engage parental interest is to provide a sensible Sunday-school program that is full of excitement and touches lives. The ways and means of attaining this goal are detailed in the following chapters.

Notes

1. *The Hymnal of the Protestant Episcopal Church, 1940* (New York: The Church Pension Fund, 1940), Hymn 298.

2. Celia Hahn and R. T. Gribbon, "Why Do People Come Back to Church?" *Action Information*, 8, no. 3 (May–June 1982): 1. (The Alban Institute, Inc., Mount St. Alban, Washington, DC 20016.)

3. *In Touch*, the newsletter of St. Paul's Episcopal Church (Sept. 20–Oct. 3, 1981), 6249 Canal Blvd., New Orleans, LA 70124, p. 4. Attributed to *Time* magazine (Los Angeles: Time Inc., n.d.), n.p. (Author's Note: I exhausted every means to verify this citation, which I think germane—not essential but helpful—to this chapter. If you, the reader, know its origin, I would be grateful for your help.)

4. Hahn and Gribbon, "Why Do People Come Back to Church?"

CHAPTER TWO

Developing the Dream
of a Great Sunday School

What is the secret of a great Sunday school? Peggy Barton and a host of others have shown me five necessary components.

MANAGING NINE MONTHS CREATIVELY

First and, I believe, most important, *the nine-month Church-school year must be divided into manageable parts.* Whereas public schools have six-week terms, three or four quarters, or two semesters, I propose five terms, drawn from the seasons of the Church year. Each runs from six to eight weeks.

The year begins in September with the All-Saints term, followed by Christmas, Epiphany, Lent, and Easter/Pentecost. This is the beginning of a good map; the nine-month journey is becoming manageable.

You may be able to come up with a better organizing principle, but in any case management is what we are talking about. You might also be disposed to say the notion of the Church year is a lucky break for us, maybe even good fortune. Some of us may even think,

> Give an infinite number of monkeys an infinite number of typewriters and one of them will come up with *King Lear,* one with the Holy Scripture, one with the Bible with one typo, and on and on and on.

But if that is all you think, you are dead wrong. Chance is infinite, but there is a lot more to life than chance. So, too, the development of the Church-year's seasons, which is a sign of God's care for us.

"Education," meaning "nurture," is one of God's fundamental ministries. The gift of the seasons is a grand sign of God's educational care.

THE BOTTOM LINE: The seasonal terms organize the nine-month teaching year by sharpening the latter's focus; they make the year manageable.

ALWAYS A CELEBRATION

Second, so that the succeeding one can begin afresh, each term must come to a clearly defined end.

Just as we put one foot in front of another to walk from place to place, so a year's study needs to be carefully paced. When we drag our feet or move too hurriedly, we tend to lose the proper pace of things.

Public schools end each of their terms with report cards and examinations. I propose this: *Term-ending festival worship provides a regular pace and occasional celebration.* (And festivals are a whole lot more fun than report cards!)

This kind of worship closes "what was" so we can all happily anticipate "what's next." I have come to expect "standing room only" on these festive occasions, and a party in the parish hall allows everyone to enjoy one another's company. Communion takes place, and love takes shape.

HAVING FUN WITH THE BIBLE

Third, *the Bible is our special book,* and learning satisfies us most when it centers on God's acts and his living presence. Parents are especially appreciative when Scripture's witness is explored.

Both the Bible and Church history provide entry into God's ministry in the "there and then" of history, whereas classroom, parish, and community life provides an opportunity to explore God's presence and ministry in the "here and now" of life.

THE POINT IS: When God's ministry and mighty acts in the past are celebrated in story, worship, and play, our eyes are opened by him to see his presence in our lives today.

Each of the five terms is an opportunity to explore God's ministry in the "there and then" of history as well as the "here and now" of everyday life. The coordination of Scripture with worship and parish life is carefully detailed in the last five chapters of this book.

INVOLVING EVERYONE

Fourth, *the whole parish needs to know what is going on in the classroom.*

When parents know what their children are doing, when they are themselves studying the same materials in adult-education programs, and when everyone worships together regularly, an enthusiastic atmosphere is generated. Everyone is drawn to participate, for the same reason that it is hard to stand by on the curb when a parade band marches by.

THE BOTTOM LINE: Christian education is best when it is consistent throughout the parish. When folks don't know what is going on, fragmentation results, and that is a far cry from communion. A coordinated ministry is required.

EXPECTING AND ENJOYING GOD'S MINISTRY

Fifth, *God is expected to be present, and signs of his presence and ministry in everyday life are known for what they are.*

Why is it necessary to pay such close attention to God's presence and ministry when we speak of organizing a parish for Christian education?

The God revealed in the "there and then" of Scripture's witness is a faithful God. Just as he stirred hearts then, so God stirs them now. Just as he illuminated minds then, so does his ministry to us today.[1]

God is a good teacher; we know he is because we know Jesus was. What is the fundamental shape of his teaching ministry? Simply to stir our hearts and illuminate our minds to his living presence.

Not to know the shape of God's ministry in the enterprise of parish education is like trying to assemble a child's Christmas present without the directions. Frustration quickly sets in, no matter how good our intentions, and anger soon follows.

THE FACT IS:When we are tuned to God's ministry and the assistance he asks of us, parish Sunday schools flourish. More than a few stories bear this point out.

Paul puts it this way: "We know that all things work together for good to them that love the Lord" (Romans 8:28). Let there be no mistake; God can work with our ignorance as well as our knowledge, but good stewardship demands as much knowledge as possible. I believe God works best with knowledge; grand Sunday-school programs bear this out.

THE RESULTS OF A GOOD SUNDAY-SCHOOL PROGRAM

What can we expect to result from a first-rate Sunday-school program?

1. When classroom studies center on the Bible, when learnings are occasionally celebrated in the Church's worship, and when everyone knows what is going on, enthusiasm—from the Greek *en* (in) *Theos* (God)—characterizes parish life; the cup of parish life begins to fill with a feeling I call "blessed."

2. A thriving Sunday-school program is high on the list of priorities of parents looking for a Church to call home. Young families naturally gravitate toward churches with good educational programs. God uses what he has to call people home to himself, and a good Sunday-school program is a ministry he uses particularly well.

3. "Standing room only" will likely characterize each term's festival worship. The house will be packed with children, teachers, parents, friends, and those newly attendant because they are invited just for the occasion. Like Christmas and Easter, term-ending festivals are used by God to build his Church.

4. A good parish educational program means an increase in pledging. The every-member canvass is easier because everyone is already involved. Excitement is contagious. Vision elicits hope, and hope gives rise to confidence and joy. The cup of parish life overflows, not because we make it happen but because the people of God put their treasure where their heart is.

Christian education is one of the most fundamental parish ministries. When it is honored for what it is, benefits accrue. God uses it to work powerful miracles, just a few of which have we noted so far.

NEWSPAPER PUBLICITY, CHRISTIAN EDUCATION, AND EVANGELISM

Let your community know what you are doing on Sunday morning. More than a few parishes keep too much of God's light "under a bushel." Christian education is one of God's finest ministries.

Let us begin by considering the term-ending festivals. Probably every child's family will be present, maybe even joined by friends and neighbors, some churched and some not. All are interested in what is going on.

At first glance it may appear that these people are attending out of curiosity or because of a personal invitation only. Another look, with eyes of faith, suggests more.

People do not come to church because they alone have decided to do so; they come because they are *called*. The apparent decision is in response to God's invitation. Though they may not consider the decision as anyone's but their own, we know better. Whether or not we choose to share their interpretation is not a fundamental issue; rather, it is our ability to offer thanks to one doing, in our lives and theirs, infinitely more than we can ask for or imagine.

Now add the following axiom to the excitement of grand worship and an enthusiastic educational program: Good copy sells papers. The newsrooms of many city and small-town newspapers are often slow on Sunday. The city editors are always looking for interesting stories to inform readers of local happenings. So if you stage a chancel drama, or get the fire fighters to help you teach on a Sunday in the fall, or celebrate a blessing of the animals in the spring, let your local newspaper know it is taking place. God uses such copy to introduce himself all the more to his world.

The word "evangelism" is rooted in the Greek *ueu angelein*, meaning "to bear good tidings." The Greek *angelein* is the root of the word "angel." The angel is a messenger.

Evangelists are messengers, too. They are not high-pressure salespersons trying to convince others to be "saved." For the most part, evangelism today is like the ministry of the angels who announced Jesus's birth to the shepherds. There was no high-pressure sales pitch then, and none is needed now.

Here is the ministry of introductions in a nutshell, though God's name may never be used in the news story. THE BOTTOM LINE IS: We are not simply talking about newspaper publicity; we are describing evangelism in the best sense of the word.

Nearly every parish lists among its members a person or two with some newspaper background who may occasionally write free-lance articles. Enlist their talents for the sake of publicizing God's ministry.

HERE IS WHAT RESULTS: Parishioners become increasingly excited about Christian education, as do others in the community. God's Church expands, for the good news is proclaimed. And it is all free!

Note

1. *The Book of Common Prayer, 1979,* p. 858.

CHAPTER THREE

One Great Big Nine-Month Celebration

BRINGING ORDER

Nine months is a long time to go without a break. As when running, it helps to take a breather every once in a while—unless you are into full-time training, and most of us aren't.

But what kind of schedule works best? Six weeks is a common pattern in the public-school system. It is the one with which most of us are acquainted, and it has proven to set a good pace. So without further ado, we could divide the nine-month school year into six-week terms—or, if that is unsatisfactory, into four-week terms, or two-month terms, and so on.

But simply being arbitrary is not really being fair with some of the tools God has given us. So before you decide on your own schedule of terms, let me introduce you to an adaptation of the historical Church year that makes a lot of sense.

This Church-year schedule offers more than just focused periods of study; automatically it relates classroom study to themes in Sunday morning's worship and provides a setting for occasional chancel drama or pageants. Thus coherence in the Sunday morning educational enterprise grows by great leaps.

ORGANIZING THE YEAR BY SEASONS

"Advent tells us Christ is near; Christmas tells us Christ is here. . . ."[1] Here is a hymn with a purpose; it has helped generations of children and adults learn about Jesus.

[15]

The Church year provides a simple and easily remembered framework for organizing any program of Christian education, whether created from scratch or using "store-bought" materials.

THE PLAIN FACT IS: The framework described above effectively focuses parish attention on the educational enterprise. When everyone knows what is going on, and it is fun, Christian education is one

GREAT,
> BIG,
>> NINE-MONTH
>> CELEBRATION.

LACK OF DIRECTION LEADS TO ANGER AND DISAPPOINTMENT

All of us need to know where we are headed. When we don't know where (and why), insecurity and anger follow as surely as the sun sets.

Peggy Barton felt this way during the one year she taught. So have many of us. The seasons of the Church year provide an organizing principle ready for use.

THE PLAIN FACT IS: As seasonal goals are set, reached, and held up for celebration, parish trust, confidence, and joy grow in great leaps. With term-ending festivals we celebrate the completion of seasonal goals, and through them we are allowed to feel God's blessing on an educational enterprise making all kinds of good sense.

FIVE SEASONAL TERMS PROVIDE TEACHING FOCUS

The schedule is really simple. Running about *six weeks each*, the terms bring everyone and everything together. *They focus parish attention* on at least one Christian theme all the time. Here indeed is coherence.

The historic Church year is easily adapted to this yearly cycle of five teaching terms. Further, each of the terms naturally accommodates the great biblical stories of God's mighty acts, of the life, death, and resurrection of Jesus, and of themes like sin and redemption, to name just some of those it is possible to study.

Beginning in September, the *All-Saints* term concentrates on what it means to be fully human and the way in which a sovereign God brings forth fresh life in his world . . . through people. All saints, all of us.

In the *Christmas* term, study centers on the fully human person of Jesus, his advent and birth. The imagery of light, from both the Old and New Testaments, provides the material, and the overwhelming impression one gathers is that God is light, yesterday, today, and forever.

The *Epiphany* term focuses on the world's appreciative response to God's light of Jesus and his gospel. The world responds favorably (Lent excepted), and the world's reply leads to a study of communion and community.

In the term of *Lent,* which follows, study narrows to the darker side of human nature and the world's hostile response to the gospel. The Easter festival of the resurrection and a sovereign God's promise of a new life caps it all off.

During *Easter/Pentecost* we search out the way in which, no matter what we do, a loving God always brings life out of dead things. Since God mostly accomplishes this goal through women and men of every generation, we are returned to the idea of sainthood.

We have thus come full cycle, and the following fall's course of study is nicely anticipated.

THE BOTTOM LINE IS: Every successful Sunday school has developed a way to focus parish attention on the educational enterprise. You may invent a way unique to your "shop," but without one your educational enterprise will probably suffer badly.

AN ADDED BONUS: With only a bit of modification, every lectionary-based curriculum easily fits into this organizing pattern. Coherence among classes and families results. A symphony develops. Organization like this does not lend itself to noise and chaos.

GOD'S PROVIDENCE MAKES THE CHURCH YEAR MANAGEABLE

It is more than chance that we have such a convenient thematic schedule. God really is with us, and the Church year is an expression of his providence and care.

The word "providence" is rooted in the Latin *pro* (for) and *video* (see). It connotes God's capacity to see ahead for us, and his ability to provide for our necessities even before we need or know we shall have need of them.

Still, some might argue that this organizing principle exists because of good luck, or good fortune, or fate.

BUT THE BOTTOM LINE IS: God is unreservedly for us, and his care is specifically shaped. The gift of the Church year is one expression of his care, providing us with a framework within which Scripture, worship, and Sunday-school classes can be organized to yield the best possible education. The progression of the Church year has been used this way for centuries. In our mobile society, with its pressures toward fragmentation, the Church year is proving to be a gift whose time has come.

KEEPING EVERYONE INVOLVED

In those parishes where Sunday school is in trouble, few people know what is happening; and even if they do know, little is known of how one component relates to another—the classroom to worship, for instance.

Parents are not clear about what their children are learning; they hear about the "fun" and wonder about the "work." Teachers miss appreciative remarks about their careful plans, and the Sunday school seems to stew alone on a little-noticed backburner. Enthusiasm and joy have a hard time taking shape in this atmosphere.

Noisy chaos is kept to a minimum when everyone knows what is going on. No news is bad news where parish Christian education is concerned.

But the seasons of the Church year provide an antidote, and here is how.

1. First, right at the beginning of September, publish a schedule of the season's terms and the major events planned for them. This takes summer planning (better even to do it the previous spring).

One parish calls its schedule *the Map.* It is brightly painted and displayed in a prominent place; No back hall or out-of-the-way place for this poster!

2. A prominently placed Christian-education bulletin board can feature seasonal displays and outlines of tasks for individual classes.

Often teachers new in the classroom wonder, "What shall my class do?" The bulletin board is one good task, along with many others (described in the chapters below on the seasons). Through these projects biblical stories can be happily explored, and at their best they are far more than mere "busy work."

The bulletin board must not be posted in the back hall of the church school; in fact, it ought to be in *the* most important place—near the church office, for instance, or in the narthex by the front doors of the church. Every parish has such a place, and that is where the Christian-education bulletin board ought to be.

This bulletin board must not be small; it must be as big as it is important, maybe four feet by ten or twelve feet. Parish Christian education isn't small, nor is the Teacher.

The board ought to be well lighted, too, and placed so people can stand and look at it. Too great a task you say? Too difficult?

THE POINT IS: Everyone likes to feel valued, and when they do, communion results. The bulletin board just described does three things: 1. It displays information about the biblical tradition; 2. It shows the class is hard at work, enjoying the Christian tradition; 3. The parish—parents, children, and teachers—gains information and knows the satisfaction of appreciative comments.

A bulletin board is simply a "detail" in any Sunday-school program, but such details make the crucial difference. Attention to detail generally separates enjoyable Sunday-school programs from those just limping along.

Pupils can use class time to create the bulletin board, learn much by developing it, and rejoice in the approbation they receive for a job well done. God uses the board as well, acquainting his people with the good work he is doing in the classroom.

Children are always proud to present something special to the parish.

I have found that when parents are clued in at regular intervals about what their children are learning and why, their appreciation and affection rubs off on the children, and the class is nicely sustained.

Conversely, when parents feel separated from their children's education, their anxiety adversely colors parish life and critical comments are voiced more frequently. This negativity seems to be the result of the parents feeling out of step with those they love and for whom they are responsible.

What I am proposing is a bulletin-board ministry that can be regularly undertaken and shared by many Sunday-school classes.

3. Publish weekly notices about current events in the classroom, or vignettes about what has happened. Keep the parish posted. This is yet another expression of God's good news, maybe not the biblical kind but very useful to God as he goes about the business of building a Christian community.

You can count on the growth of interest and enthusiasm as the good news spreads.

For parish Christian education, no news is bad news.

USE OF SEASONAL COLORS

Colors greatly enhance classroom teaching and term-ending festivals; they give visual expression to seasonal themes.

In Protestant denominations, including the Episcopal Church, there are no rubrics or canons governing the use of colors; it is a matter of both general and local custom.

A growing number of parishes are giving the task of constructing bright banners, vestments, and altar hangings to their Church-school classes. Festival worship is thereby nicely enhanced. Such a task also provides a splendid opportunity for intergenerational learning, as young and old, singles and families gather together to share common goals—to create something splendid and to prepare for participation in an impending festival.

The use of colors in Christian worship began before historical reference to it. We know a sequence of colors was in use in Jerusalem by the late twelfth century: Black was used at Christmas and for festivals of Mary, the mother of Jesus; blue was used for the Epiphany and Ascension, perhaps because the color of the sky suggests the universality of the good news of God's joining with us in Christ Jesus. Who knows?

By the end of the twelfth century, Pope Innocent III had apparently persuaded the general Church to adopt the color sequence of red, white, green, and violet.

In medieval England, our forebears constructed the finest and newest of vestments for use at the great feasts. Plain or older vestments were used for the ordinary worship of the "house." Sackcloth was used during Lent, colors on other occasions.

THE POINT IS: Colors are vehicles of communication; they give seasonal expression to the faith of the Church, and designing banners and hangings generates the kind of Christian fellowship that makes for splendid parish life.

Notes

1. *The Hymnal of the Protestant Episcopal Church, 1940* (New York: The Church Pension Fund, 1940), Hymn 235.
2. Ibid., Hymn 243.

CHAPTER FOUR

Faith's Birth and Christian Education

This chapter and the next describe God's ministry in the Sunday-school classroom. It is derived from the experience of people just like you and me.

Christian education is definable, but merely to do so is irresponsible without a working consideration of what God is up to in the enterprise.

So, then, just how does God participate in the Sunday-school enterprise? It is a question all of us ought to be able to answer. Complex, you say? Not so.

God's fundamental ministry—according to Scripture and as experience shows it—is faith's birth and growth, in us.

The stories cited in this chapter are meant to paint vivid pictures of God's ministry and faith's development, and they are the best way I know to begin to define Christian education and to detail what it is supposed to accomplish.

LEWIS GREEN'S SUNDAY-MORNING CLASS

I have listened to more than a few stories about what adults remember from their childhood Sunday-school years, and they all, every one, affirm the same thing—what we remember most is *being loved by a teacher who mattered to us.* Those teachers, every one of them, represented God, and through them God met us.

Steven's story, below, makes exactly this point. As you read it, keep in mind the question, "What's going on here?" and God will provide some answers that make sense to you.

When I was ten years old, I was "recruited" into Lewis Green's Sunday school class. I say "recruited" because Lewis was an ex-marine drill sergeant turned newspaper reporter and Sunday school teacher.

My older brother and some of his friends had preceded me in this venture, and their activities were a source of wonder to me, fueling my desire to belong. It was my brother's friend who finally convinced both my brother and Lewis that this skinny little kid had the makings of a raw recruit. Thus, I became a life-long member of the church school regiment that called itself the Unsophisticated Meatballs.

I was given the rank of buck private and told that there were expectations on my life which, if adhered to, would result in my rising through the ranks in due time.

The "Unsophisticated Meatballs" met on Sunday morning as did other classes, and did some typical things like Bible study and singing. However, I cannot remember any of the specifics of what we learned in those class sessions. But I do remember that Lewis ran a tight ship.

I remember even more the frequent camping trips to Lewis's favorite wilderness, a place called Wild Cat Cliffs. Lewis was also a great storyteller, and I can remember sitting around the campfire in the dark nights at Wild Cat Cliffs, being scared out of my wits by stories like "The Ghost Who Lost His Golden Leg."

Some of our camping trips were all weekend affairs which, I remember, caused a lot of conflict in the parish. "Why aren't the kids in church this Sunday?" was one refrain.

Lewis was not too popular with the more traditional Sunday school teachers, but I recall that the more abuse he suffered, the more we all rallied to his cause.

Over the course of four years I rose in the ranks to technical sergeant, and received several printed certificates saying that the following person has been "declared an Unsophisticated Meatball in good standing and has achieved the rank of . . . on this day. . . ."

Like I said, I've long since forgotten what Lewis Green taught me about being religious, but I've never forgotten that I belonged to a special community, and grew in my identity through that experience. It was my first experience of an intensive fellowship in which I was given a Name and a Purpose. In it I knew that I was part of the Kingdom in a special way. I was being moved, scared, and challenged, seized by a purpose larger than myself. There was preparation for the future, there was an experience of common growth in the Gospel, although I would not have named it so at the time (and many others would not have either).

Full awareness of my growth came better than twenty years after my graduation from that class. I ran into another Meatball whom I had not seen since childhood. He remembered too. And he said there were others who had never forgotten either.

God met us then like now, though we never thought much of it at the time. Looking back, I now see lots of similar times, unnoted in the moment, but full of God's presence though never named.

The word "conversation" is rooted in the Latin, meaning "to travel with." God keeps conversational company with every one of us. He walks with us and talks with us, and though we may never hear a voice, along the road of life we are converted, gently for the most part, into a trusting reliance on his presence and ministry.

God stood at the door of this young man's life and knocked (Revelation 3:20), and God became flesh in the life of Lewis Green. God also suffered, I suspect, as his ministry through Lewis Green was occasionally misunderstood, but God was not deterred. His is a faithful ministry to us.

The First Thing We Learn Is: More than simply teaching information about God (as important as that is), we Sunday-school teachers must first help God bind the children of the world to himself. This seems to be God's fundamental ministry in Sunday-morning Christian education.

PARENTAL HOPES AND EXPECTATIONS

When asked about what they hope Sunday school will offer their children, most parents say things like
—"knowledge of God," or
   —"I hope they'll learn what's in the Bible," or
      —"I hope they'll begin to have faith."
What we have here are *two sets of hopes and expectations*. Both are important, but they are also different.

One set of expectations has to do with *increased knowledge* about who God is and what the Bible has to say about him. This is intellectual learning. (This first group of expectations and ways to meet them are developed in the next chapter.)

The second set of expectations centers on *the development of faith and belief,* the subject of this chapter's discussion.

THIS CHAPTER'S POINT: The birth and growth of faith and biblical knowledge about God are closely related and both are important, but they are not identical. The latter we can do something about, but the former lies primarily in the province of God's care and ministry to us.

GOD'S MINISTRY: SIMPLY BEING WITH ALL OF US

Emblazoned high above the altar in the Immanuel Chapel of Virginia Theological Seminary is the Great Commission of Mark's Gospel,

"GO YE INTO ALL THE WORLD AND PREACH THE GOSPEL"

(Mark 16:5)

In my student days at that seminary, I (and many others) used to wrestle about what the gospel, boiled down to its essentials, might be. Each of us had some basic answer, but none satisfied.

Then one day I made a connection between the name of the chapel, Immanuel, meaning "God with us," and the Great Commission. The good news of Jesus is that God is with us, right now. I have never lost that vision.

And here, too, is the vision, lying right at the center of any consideration of Christian education: God is with us, and he is not passive.

POINT: We can depend on God's interested participation anytime Christian education takes place, doing, as Paul puts it, "infinitely more than we can ask for or imagine"[1] (Ephesians 3.20).

God's "withness" is clearly present in the story of Lewis Green's class. Even though material like biblical stories is not explicitly remembered by Steven, God was doing infinitely more among them than he or his classmates knew.

What resulted from God's presence in the lives of Lewis Green's children? They were bound more closely to God, though during their camping trips he was, perhaps, the farthest thought from their minds.

Events like these are common to all Christian Education programs, although often unnoticed and little valued.

THE MINISTRY OF GOD'S HOLY SPIRIT TO HUMAN SPIRIT

God will not be denied joining with us in life. Whether we like it or not, God enjoys being with us. He knows the number of hairs on our heads (Matthew 10:30, Luke 12:7), his everlasting arms are always under us (Deuteronomy 33:27), and it was his wind alone that brought humankind to life (Genesis 2:7).

Below Hans Kung describes the presence of God's spirit and its effect in our lives. The feminine pronoun is used to speak of God's Holy Spirit in this section, although Kung does not use it in his work.

> Perceptible and yet not perceptible, invisible and yet powerful, real like the energy-charged air, the wind, the storm, as important for life as the air we breathe: this is how people in ancient times frequently imagined the "Spirit" and God's invisible working.
>
> According to the beginning of the creation account, "spirit" (Hebrew, *ruah*; Greek, *pneuma*) is the "roaring," the "tempest" of God over the waters. . . .
>
> "Spirit" as understood in the Bible means the force or power proceeding from God, which is opposed to "flesh," to created, perishable reality: that invisible force of God and power of God which is effective creatively or destructively, for life or judgment in creation and in history, in Israel and in the Church. [God's Spirit] comes upon [us] powerfully or gently, stirring up individuals or even groups to ecstasy, often effective in extraordinary phenomena, in great men and women, in Moses and the "judges" of Israel, in warriors and singers, kings, prophets and prophetesses.
>
> This Spirit, then, is not—as the word itself might well suggest— the spirit of [humankind], [our] knowing and willing living self. [She] is the Spirit of God, who as Holy Spirit is sharply distinguished from the unholy spirit of [humankind] and the world. . . .
>
> The spirit is no other than God himself: God close to [humankind] and the world, as comprehending but not comprehensible, self-bestowing but not controllable, life-giving but also directive power and force. [She] is then not a third party, not a thing between God and [us], but God's personal closeness . . . to us.[2]

God is close, and he touches us in many ways. Faith's development in the Sunday-school classroom illustrates this point well.

Human consciousness can be thought of as divided into three parts:

1. *Consciousness,* or what we know and what we are consciously aware of.
2. *Semi-consciousness,* or what we suspect and sense.

3. *Unconsciousness,* or what we don't consciously know but of
   which we are nevertheless deeply aware.

Though artificial, these distinctions help us appreciate the deeply pervasive way God is with us.

Consciousness is what we know, what we see, hear, taste, feel,
and understand. Lewis Green's students were conscious of good times
and fun, of feelings of fellowship and joy, but few of them were then
aware that God was touching them, and none of them then knew it
quite the way Steven knows it now.

But there is more to life than what we consciously know. Just as
most of an iceberg lies below the surface of the sea, so does most of
us lie below our awareness.

At the *semi-conscious* and *unconscious* levels God was also stirring
those students' hearts and minds to his presence. He was building in
them a knowledge that not only did Lewis Green care but he, God,
cared as well. God used every one of those times to bond those
children more closely to himself, building in each case a personal
relationship.

Not that God is ever not with us. But given our limited openness
to his presence, we know his touch only now and then. Still, at deeper
levels we sense it all the more, and consequently we are confident
that the world, though stretched between the poles of "for better"
and "for worse," is still more "for better."

God's touch and announcement begin the process of calling us
into relationship—whether we consciously know it or not. Bonds of
relationship are slowly built, and natural faith begins its birth. The
world is seen as trustworthy because there is a friend present in our
lives, one whom we know because he has revealed himself, even
though we may not yet know his name.

THE BIRTH OF FAITH

Faith is the natural human response to God's presence and ministry in our lives. Faith is not what we *believe* about God, for belief
has more to do with knowledge *about* God. Nor is it something we
give to, or get from, one another. Faith has to do with trust, security,
and confidence, and it springs only from the touch of God immediately
present in our lives. Hence, the task of Christian education is that of
pointing out the signs of God's presence and ministry, so that folks
can see them and, seeing, perhaps trust all the more deeply.

John Westerhoff makes exactly this point:

> Faith cannot be taught by any method of instruction; we can only
> teach religion. We can know about religion, but we can only expand
> in faith, act in faith, live in faith.
>
> Faith can be inspired within the community of faith, but it cannot
> be given to one person by another.
>
> An emphasis on school and instruction makes it too easy to forget
> this truth. It encourages us to teach about Christian religion by
> turning our attention to Christianity as expressed in documents, doc-
> trines, history and moral codes.
>
> [This] leads us to focus on religion rather than faith.[3]

The Hebrew roots of the word "faith" are *amen* and *batah*. *Amen*
has to do with a sense of solidity and sureness, and *batah* suggests
an attitude of security and confidence. The word "confidence" is
rooted in the Latin *con* and *fidere*, and means "to stand with." When
God stands with us and we are privileged to know it, responding to
his interested knock (Revelation 3:20), faith takes shape. We begin to
sense the presence of another, though not yet knowing his biblical
identity (only Scripture provides that knowledge). But we sense a
companionable presence, and we feel secure and confident. At precisely this point faith is born.

Signs of what I call *amen* and *batah* faith are readily apparent in
Lynn's story:

> Although I know I regularly attended Sunday school during my
> early years, I cannot remember any specifics.
>
> I do, however, remember Joe. He was a sexton in one of my
> Dad's early parishes. Many's the time I'd help Joe with his work,
> during Sunday school hours and otherwise.
>
> I liked being with Joe. I listened to him as we pushed mops, set
> chairs and emptied waste cans. Joe told me bible stories I can hear
> to this day, and he related them to the events of life in the world.
> He shared with me his joy in the Lord, his pain, his frustrations,
> his faith and questions. He laughed a lot, and sometimes he cried.
> And he sang a lot. Lord, did [we] sing.
>
> Joe was strong and he was conscientious. And he disciplined me
> when I was lazy in my assigned work.
>
> If it's not already apparent, Joe was also my friend. He always
> had time for me, and the patience to enjoy it.
>
> I loved Joe. And I'll always remember him. He was a disciple of
> Jesus, and his ecstasy and joy in the Lord brought God's presence
> close and made it real.

God met me in that relationship, though I'd have never said so then. I simply didn't know all that was happening.

THE POINT IS: Faith is not a commodity to be given; it is the natural human response to God's presence in our lives. God gives us his presence, and the human response is what we call faith, a sort of awareness that there is "more around me, and in me, than me."

God has nothing better to do than to be with us; all Scripture bears this witness. Though God is always present, we are not always aware that he is touching our lives. But that is not necessary for faith's development.

TWO STYLES OF FAITH: NATURAL AND CHRISTIAN

I have listened to many recollections of childhood experiences in Sunday school, and I have discovered two styles of faith, both of which are important. One style of faith I call *natural* and the other *Christian*. The latter is often valued more highly than the former, though the former is supremely important and always fundamental.

Natural faith is the natural human response to God's presence and ministry in our lives. The sense of peace and satisfaction filling Lynn's life is the shape of natural faith.

One does not have to be a Christian to feel such things. God meets us where we are, just as we are.

Long before the children in Lewis Green's classroom acquired much explicit knowledge about God, they felt love, security, and confidence—gifts only God can give.

But when God is present and known by his biblical identity to be present, *Christian faith* takes shape.

If you want children to begin the journey toward Christian faith, put them in places where God is known to be present—like Lewis Green's classroom. One cannot guarantee Christian faith's birth—that is between God and the child—but we can plant the lives of our children in growth-stimulating environments like the Christian Church, for Christian faith is more likely to develop there than not.

THE BOTTOM LINE: When God is present in our lives and felt by us to be present, natural faith is born. When we know God's identity, using Scripture's witness, Christian faith is shaped. We need to look for, and rejoice in, both styles of faith, particularly as we plan for Christian education, for both are gifts generated by God's presence and ministry in our midst.

NATURAL FAITH BECOMING CHRISTIAN

For most of us, natural faith is transformed into Christian faith in the Church.

Because children experience good feelings and a sense of fellowship within a community called Christian, natural faith gradually becomes Christian. How does this happen? By our simply suspecting that God and Jesus have something to do with what is happening— simply because we talk about them so much—children soon begin to make connections between the biblical stories and their own lives.

Christian faith takes explicit shape when we are able to say something like this: "I am never alone, for God, who showed himself in Christ, is with me."

In the following story you will plainly see the birth and growth of natural faith and, over the course of years, natural faith slowly becoming Christian.

Jane describes faith's growth this way:

> Sunday was a special day in my family. What set it apart was the fact that without fail our family attended Sunday services regularly, during the school year as well as on vacation.
>
> Each summer our family vacationed for three months at our beach cottage on the Atlantic coast of North Carolina. On Sundays we children put on "Sunday clothes," and struggled to get our sunburned feet back into now-tight shoes.
>
> After gathering up all the children in the neighborhood, my father drove our full car across the long bridge to the mainland. There, in a tiny whitewashed church, we'd have an opening time of fellowship singing hymns like, "He Leadeth Me, O Blessed Thought." It was a big gathering, adults and children together. Then we children would be herded off by age groups to Sunday school classes.
>
> When church was over, all of us hopped in the car and headed for the beach. Then came the really big treat of the day. My father always stopped at a grocery store owned by a Mr. Barefoot. The name always struck me as very appropriate for the beach.
>
> And all of us were treated to a popsicle. Here was our after-Sunday-school ritual, standing outside Mr. Barefoot's, by now shoeless again, and me with an orange popsicle dripping all down the front of my Sunday dress in the hot North Carolina sun.
>
> I cannot remember much about what I "learned" in that tiny little whitewashed church. What I do remember is the habit of churchgoing, even during vacation. I still go to church year 'round.
>
> This cumulative childhood experience is one of my greatest leg-

acies from my parents. It put meaning for me into the Fourth Commandment from early on, "Remember the Sabbath day to keep it holy . . . the Lord blessed the Sabbath day and hallowed it."

Somehow, though I didn't know it then, God was also hallowing me, making me a bit more whole as a child of His.

I understand Mr. Barefoot still runs that small store in Nags Head, North Carolina. To this day he may be unaware of his participation in God's ministry of binding this woman to himself more than four decades ago.

THE BOTTOM LINE: With a little support from parents, children move easily from natural faith to a deeper and more personal faith in God's love and care for them.

Stories like those quoted above encourage an appreciation for the majestic and wide-ranging ministry of Christian education, the tenderness of faith's birth, and the patience of God's ministry to us.

CHRISTIAN FAITH'S GROWTH IN THE CLASSROOM

The growth of Christian faith is, for most of us, slow.

In the following story, Nancy looks back at an early Sunday-school experience. Through her retrospection we are privileged to see Christian faith taking shape in the life of a little girl, though many years ago she did not (indeed, could not) conceive it as such. Happily, God is at work nevertheless.

Thinking back to childhood Sunday school, I'm surprised with the experience I remember best and most positively. It is not an experience of song or paper or paste, nor is it an experience of playing or laughing or storytelling. It is an experience of discipline, order and responsibility. It is the experience of Mrs. Snow's third grade.

In the church where I grew up, children did not attend worship with the adults until after the third grade. Toddlers up to the third grade stayed in Sunday school for the entire morning. A separate children's service, about 20 minutes length, was part of our morning's activities.

By the time I was in the third grade, I was eager to leave the little children behind and go to church with the big folks. Going to the adult service symbolized my maturity and "grown-up-ness."

But Mrs. Snow had other plans for "her" third grade, and for me. And I remember it yet.

She expected us to set examples for the younger children. She believed that as the oldest children in the children's service, we should show those younger how to act in church. I remember specifically how she taught us to kneel, knees bent of course, and no slouching or sitting. We were also to hold our hands clasped in prayer. She went over the service with us so that we knew the many parts from memory.

Her teaching how to pray in church stayed with me. Even today when I rest on the pew while kneeling, I remember times long ago.

My experience with Mrs. Snow might appear to some as negative. Not so. Mrs. Snow made me feel good about myself. She made me feel important. I became excited about my new responsibilities to set examples for others. I was pleased as well with the idea that I was old enough to carry myself with poise and respect, and I sensed her pride and concern for me.

Mrs. Snow related to us as adults, or at least that was how we felt she was relating to us. Her action toward me was important in making me feel more mature.

Third grade was a major transition for me. I was prepared by Mrs. Snow for a change, a passage into the adult world. Outwardly Mrs. Snow encouraged us to adopt a proper prayer posture and mature, attentive behavior in church. And inwardly we felt different as well. Sensing her respect, we valued ourselves all the more.

The New Testament Greek word we translate "transfiguration" is also the basis of the word metamorphosis. Indeed, Mrs. Snow saw us coming out of the cocoon. And she made us feel and act like grateful, beautiful butterflies.

This third grader is now an adult—and a priest in the Church of God.

WHAT WE LEARN IS: Christian faith takes shape as children connect what they are experiencing with what they are studying.

THE BOTTOM LINE: Christian educators can count on God's presence and ministry in everyday life, particularly in the classroom. We teach neither alone nor in a vacuum; another is present, already stirring hearts and illumining minds. We are simply called to participate in his preexistent ministry.

One last story helps make this point:

A while back I participated with a group of five and six year olds learning about Communion. I was a member of their congregation.

I was particularly impressed by the way the presiding priest was able to help shape their enthusiasm and interest, not pushing too much information, but depending upon and using their curiosity as bread and wine were handled. There was a lot more commotion than 11 o'clock Sunday's worship, but it was not at all disrespectful.

What I saw most of all was this. In the hubbub of twisting bodies, questions, and an occasional punch or two as room was made at the rail, I saw the marketplace of life, and above it all I heard the words, "The body of our Lord Jesus Christ keep you in everlasting life." The children heard it too, perhaps through ears smaller than mine, but amplified by God's presence in their lives.

Natural faith's development was clearly evident in their fellowship and joy, and as well I felt my own faith teased to life.

But are there any signs of the belief that begins to characterize the faith we call Christian? I think so, but the truth of it only later surfaced.

Later the same day, one of these six year olds wanted to join his nine year old brother at a late afternoon movie. Since mom and dad were already committed to something else, they said "no," not wanting the boys in the shopping mall all by themselves. But the boys persisted, and finally the youngest—who'd participated in the communion service just that morning, pulled his trump: "But we won't be alone, Jesus will be with us."

Chuckle if you will, but there is a mystery here: Added to natural faith is knowledge of God, and at precisely this point natural faith is becoming Christian faith.

God is always about the business of touching our lives, and when we begin to talk about his presence and ministry, deep within us he whispers, "It's true."

CHRISTIAN FAITH DEFINED

Whenever we begin to believe that another, higher power is the God of Abraham and Sarah, Isaac and Rebecca, Jacob and Rachel, and the God and Father of our Lord Jesus Christ, Christian faith begins to take shape.

This is what makes natural faith Christian: The growing belief that Jesus is the only perfect image of the Father, and shows us the nature of God.[4]

If there is any one goal for Christian education, it is the development of Christian faith. As we have seen, however, faith's birth and growth lies within the realm of God's ministry. We certainly can help it along, but we help best by creating an environment wherein God is known to be present. Hence, we use biblical stories, worship, and prayer.

THE BOTTOM LINE: We are of course made Christian at baptism, whether as adults or infants, but we become believing Christians when natural faith is shaped by the witness of Scripture and the New Testament. Good Sunday-morning Christian education never diminishes the former and always seeks to develop the latter.

BIBLE-IMAGINATIVE SPECULATION

Pointing out the signs of God's presence and ministry in the here and now of everyday life is the best kind of Christian education. I call this method of teaching "Bible-imaginative speculation," and it is found only in *Creative Christian Education.*

Each time stories are told in this book, whether from Scripture or everyday life, Bible-imaginative speculation is the tool used to "get at" some of the less obvious, the hidden things taking place in the lives of God's people. Words like "Immanuel," "presence," "wind," and "providence" are just a few of those used to describe God's acts. You doubtless have favorite words of your own, already present to make this tool work for you.

Whenever I am responsible for Christian education in a parish, I am careful to use these meaningful words regularly, explaining them along the way. Once they are introduced, they are reinforced by Scripture, prayer, and hymn. All of us are the more deeply engaged by God, who uses these simple tools to say simply, "It's true."

Bible-imaginative speculation assumes that God acts in the here and now of everyday life just as he acted in the there and then of Scripture's witness—a legitimate assumption, because God is, of all things, faithful.

Therefore, Bible-imaginative speculation pays careful attention to stories. By using what God has chosen to reveal to us of his presence and ministry in Scripture, it can help identify signs of his presence and ministry in everyday life.

It works this way: Choose any story, and raise these two questions about it: (1) What is God's ministry here, and (2) what signs of his presence can I see? Then consider the story from the perspectives of Scripture's witness and of Church history. But make no mistake: It is not your imagination alone that satisfies; it is the dialogue of holy spirit and human spirit that is illuminating.

St. Paul enjoyed this ministry more than a few times. His use of Bible-imaginative speculation took bright shape at Athens (Acts 17:16–39):

> Paul was a stranger in town, and he found himself provoked that no one knew God, the God of Abraham and Sarah, and the God and Father of the Lord Jesus Christ.
>
> But how to make an introduction? He could get their attention by condemning their lack of belief, or by telling them they were wrong or even ignorant. But quite likely they'd have run him out of town.
>
> So Paul used a ministry of imaginative speculation, and what he did was this. He found an object around which a conversation could be built, and began to offer a sensitive interpretation from Bible perspectives.
>
> And this story of the "Altar to an Unknown God" has intrigued generations of Christians across the centuries.

Bible-imaginative speculation takes that which is available and offers an immediate interpretation from the perspective of Scripture. It offers the world the possibility of Christian faith's birth. And that is just what happened as this story in Acts concludes, for we leave Paul responding to some people newly interested in what he had to say about God.

The nurture of Christian faith in many ways depends on our ability to identify and celebrate signs of God's presence and ministry in the here and now of everyday life, and Bible-imaginative speculation commends itself to every Christian.

THE BOTTOM LINE: Merely to urge people to believe in God without helping them see in their lives the signs of God's presence and ministry is like offering a stone to those seeking the bread of life.

NURTURE AND CONVERSION IN THE CLASSROOM

The end of good Sunday-morning Christian education is conversion, and the means to that end is nurture.

Conversion is rooted in the Latin *con* and *vertus*, meaning "to turn toward" something of greater worth. God is always with us, and because of his presence natural faith naturally takes shape. Each time we respond to God's inviting knock at the door of our lives (Revelation 3:20), we turn a little bit more to him; we can't help it.

Conversion often is not a dramatic transformation, and we do ourselves and the notion a disservice by conceiving it that way only.

Though what happened to Paul on the road to Damascus happens to some of us, you won't find it happening very often in the Sunday-school classroom. If you expect to find it there, or figure you are unsuccessful if it doesn't happen, then you are going to be in for chronic disappointment.

In the Sunday-school classroom, conversion generally takes a shape like that of Jane's summer experience on the outer banks of North Carolina. God was touching Jane's life during every one of those vacations. And not just then but from the time sperm and ovum restored the species number and she was conceived in the womb. There is not ever a time God is not with us.

At the beginning of things Jane did not know it was the God of the Hebrews and the God and Father of our Lord Jesus Christ who was present with her in her life. She was, however, beginning to feel that the universe was more companionable than hostile, and she felt it only because the universe belongs to him. It was over the course of months and years, living with her family and joining with God's community of faith, that Jane first began to sense, and later to know, the identity of the one with her.

THE BOTTOM LINE: Conversion in the classroom mostly takes a gentle shape. Often we cannot see it, but God can, and that's our joy. Further, this conversion, or turning-toward-God, takes place not only at conscious levels but at semi-conscious and unconscious levels as well. God is always about the special business of touching our lives in ways we cannot begin to fathom. And the Sunday-school classroom is one important place wherein natural faith begins to become Christian.

The word *nurture* connotes the suckling of an infant at its mother's breast. It also connotes feeding generally.

Let us return to the story of Jane. She was never apart from God's care and interest, though only later did she come to know, consciously, that they were gifts from him. In early childhood Jane may have ascribed her feeling of being loved and valued to her parents. They loved her, and because of their love she was learning she was special. Or she may have included in her list of those who loved her a few siblings, or friends, or teachers, or countless others.

THE POINT IS: Underneath this rich constellation of persons we find the presence of another who cares, encouraging our growth by keeping close, encouraging, and conversational company. God is deeply involved in our growth and nurture.

The *relationship of nurture and conversion* is readily apparent in the story of Lewis Green's classroom and in Jane's reflection on her childhood summers at the beach.

Nurture preceded conversion in both instances. Yet it is clear that while the process of nurture was taking place so was that of conversion. Both children were being called by God and were turning toward him long before they were aware of what was happening. In the course of years—and these events are mere moments along the way—Jane and Stephen were being formed as Christian persons long before they had any idea of what was happening.

These insights offer the Sunday-school teacher two important perspectives, both of which lead to greater satisfaction:

1. God actively nurtures our growing up, and natural faith, because of his interest, is always taking shape. By providing a classroom atmosphere of exploration and discovery, natural faith begins to become Christian.

2. Because of God's presence and ministry, we have every reason to expect conversion to take place. It probably won't be like St. Paul's, though it may assume a more dramatic shape in some cases than others. But signs of it abound.

We are alive throughout ourselves to God's presence as one always near to us, distinct from us, but as close as breath is to the lungs.

CHRISTIAN EDUCATION'S TWO TASKS

THE PLAIN FACT IS: When God and God's people meet, and God's people know it, there is Christian education at its very best. There, too, is the beginning of Christian faith. Every story we have cited points toward this conclusion.

Thus, two tasks emerge as the work of the Christian education.

Its *first task* is to acknowledge God's presence and to expect to participate in faith's birth and growth. That is the task of celebration, which leads in the Sunday school to an atmosphere of anticipation and joy. This is the easiest of the two tasks, simply because we are respondents to God's initiative.

POINT: God is the fundamental actor in Christian education. When we know the shape of his ministry, everything else falls into place.

Christian education's *second task*—and it is a close second but second nevertheless—is that of communicating information about who God is by using the Bible and other theological resources. This is a ministry of introductions, and it is the next chapter's subject.

Both tasks go hand in hand—that is clear from all the above stories—but Christian education works best when they are valued in the order given.

CHRISTIAN EDUCATION AS A MINISTRY OF INTRODUCTIONS

Introducing God's people to God is another way to look at the task of the Sunday-morning classroom. The word "introduction" is rooted in the Latin *intro* and *ducere*, "to lead into" or "to bring to," especially for the first time. People come to church only because God invites them and they are interested. They don't decide by themselves to come to church, nor to involve their children in Sunday school; God is always a part of the deliberations leading to our decisions. There the ministry of Holy Spirit to human spirit can be felt, particularly at deep, unconscious levels.

The church of God is a people called together, and that parents and children are already in church on Sunday morning is bell-clear testament to God's inherent ministry.

God always introduces himself. At our best, then, we teachers simply provide an opportunity for the people of God to begin to meet him as the Church met him in the past, using biblical stories, prayer, and worship, and the tool of Bible-imaginative speculation.

GUARDING AGAINST TEACHER BURNOUT

All of us are too much directed by what we remember of public school. "What we remember" is an important phrase, because "what we remember" might not be the way it was but only the way we conceived it at the time. All too easily we link secular education's formal instruction, with its emphasis on textbook learning, to Sunday-school Christian education.

Many Sunday-school teachers too easily fall into the trap of emphasizing facts at the expense of valuing God's presence and faith's development. Some Sunday-morning programs have even resorted to tests and closely graded examinations!

It is one thing to introduce God and to communicate information about him; it is altogether another thing to push that information forcibly.

The American school works well to mass produce a literate citizenry, but it is not a good model for Christian education, for it encourages us to give top priority to information, to which all else is subordinated.

So why is the public-school model so compelling? Two reasons: First, we have all grown up with it, and second, clergy tend to push it. The roots of the first reason are obvious, but the roots of the second are hidden.

Residential theological education for future clergy is full-time, five days a week for a nine-month scholastic year. The medium of the seminary classroom dictates, to clergy, that Christian education is best when it is classroom-centered.

This means because of the public school's clear bias and clergy expectations, many Sunday-school teachers push *information* about God, and too few value God's ministry of faith's development.

As student boredom increases—because Sunday school is made little different from the five-day-a-week public school—teachers, wanting to be faithful and successful, tend to push even more information. And what happens? Student behavior degenerates and teachers end up feeling guilty as class attendance drops off.

I have heard more than a few "war stories" from burned-out teachers, who often feel they have let down the parish, the schoolchildren, and maybe even God. It does *not* have to be this way.

What we need to do is keep the public-school model in its place— the public school.

It is important to communicate information about God and God's Church in Sunday-school Christian education, but it must always remain secondary to our keen interest in the birth of Christian faith.

THE BOTTOM LINE: First, we Christian educators must be about the task of valuing faith's development. Second, we need to be about the task of imaginatively communicating information about God, using the Bible's witness. And these two fundamentals have to be approached in that order.

What we Christians know best is that faith is not given by one person to another; it is a gift from God, who is always present in our lives.

Notes

1. *The Book of Common Prayer, 1979*, p. 60.
2. Hans Kung, *On Being a Christian* (Garden City, New York: Doubleday and Company, 1976), 468, 489. (Author's note: I am aware of how often books—including this one—and journals refer to God in the masculine. The biblical tradition justifying this stance is very old but acknowledgment of the feminine in the Godhead is just as ancient.

Though Father and Son are firmly set, the Holy Spirit of God is referred to in scripture as both he and she. The feminine Hebrew *ruach*, breath of God, encourages Christian thought in this direction, and Jesus describes himself as a hen wanting to gather her brood, Jerusalem, under her wing (Matthew 23:37–39, Luke 13:34–35).

Because learning is such a powerful event, today's Christian education needs to recapture these rich biblical descriptions of God, for such images cannot but help serve our 20th century hope for increased respect and generosity between women and men. More assistance is found in Chapter 13, in the section headed "Mother's Day and Father's Day.")
3. John H. Westerhoff, III, *Will Our Children Have Faith?* (New York: The Seabury Press, 1976), 23.
4. *The Book of Common Prayer, 1979*, p. 849.

CHAPTER FIVE

Imaginative Bible Study

Imagine this: A fifth-grade class throws Daniel to the lions, and imagine it happening in the midst of Sunday morning's main worship. Also imagine the lively preparations for the play. After it's over and the spontaneous applause dies out, can you imagine the number of adults and children who may never forget it?

Imaginative Bible study and experiential education go hand in hand. Their task is simply to:

—set folks free to explore the Bible creatively,

—experience God's presence, and

—celebrate God's ministry.

In this open atmosphere, God touches the hearts and minds of everyone involved, and natural faith grows and Christian faith deepens.

EXPERIENTIAL EDUCATION

Experiential education is simply one way to describe the way in which we are met by God and begin to learn who he is. When something is experienced, we understand it better, we remember it better, and we feel compelled to ask questions about it.

As an ancient Chinese proverb puts it:

I hear and I forget.

I see and I remember.

I do and I understand.

POINT: Biblical stories constitute most of the content of every good Christian-education program, and they are the kinds of stories on which experiential education thrives. When the Bible is experientially explored, true conversion (discussed in the previous chapter) begins.

THE BOTTOM LINE: The *secret of a creative Sunday-school classroom* is the use of experiential education.

THE ENJOYABLE CLASS

Some brief definitions help expand the notion of experiential education. The word *education* denotes the activity of raising the young as they mature into adulthood. Education is what parents "live" with their children. Family life is a powerful educational force. So, too, is the Church-school classroom. We noted the power of both family life and the classroom in the preceding chapter.

The word *school* does not entail the classroom model of orderly desks and students quietly at work; rather, it has to do with the Latin *schola,* meaning "leisure," which time is spent discussing new information and ideas. It is akin to the Greek *echein,* meaning "to hold." A Church school, then, might be conceived of as a place where we are "held" and personally engaged so that we can grow up fully into persons who love and know the Lord.

Learning is the acquisition of knowledge and understanding. A familiar enough definition, but the word is rooted in the Latin *lira,* meaning "to furrow," suggesting the process of turning over the earth. As Scripture is turned over and looked at, appreciated and engaged, learning takes place.

Teaching has to do with the activity of showing, with a keen interest in building a person's capacity to understand. Teaching is not a coercive but an illuminative activity. As subject matter is turned over, as in furrowing, students begin to grasp the idea held up for illumination and exploration, for the ideas themselves grasp and hold their interest.

The term *experiential* has to do with trying. It is rooted in the Latin *experiri,* meaning "to try something new" that might be a bit threatening, something that expands our inner horizons.

THE BOTTOM LINE: Experiential education is a way to make the Bible come alive in the Sunday-morning classroom, even if there are only a few minutes in which to do it.

TELL STORIES, DON'T TEACH LESSONS

Children remember stories best, not lessons . . . and so do most adults. Stories like
—Daniel tossed to the lions,
—Noah building the ark,
—Jesus healing the blind Bartimaeus,
—Paul on the Damascus road,
—Jesus with his friends Mary and Martha, and
—Naomi and Ruth, Jesus's forebears.
Adults may well remember a lesson on love based on I Corinthians 13, but children will learn of love much better by reading stories like that of the Good Samaritan (Luke 10:33) or that of the love between Ruth and Naomi (Book of Ruth).

Why are stories so important? And why is the Bible full of them? Tales, fables, and personal stories are the food on which the individual personality is nourished. They convey knowledge of "how it was" so we can perceive "how it is."

POINT: Biblical stories are the windows we need to see God's presence and ministry in our lives today.

There is no better example of a story's power and God's use of it than the recollection of Jesus' Last Supper with his friends. Stories bring hope and sound warnings, and remembering the Last Supper at Sunday's Communion points out how God meets us yet.

CHOOSING BIBLICAL STORIES FOR STUDY

How do we go about choosing biblical stories for study? Each of us has his or her favorites, but what happens after they are exhausted? Fortunately, lots of help is available.

You may have heard the word "lection" used in relation to the Bible lessons used in Christian worship. A lection is a reading, and a liturgical (worship) lectionary is a list of Bible readings covering the full range of Scripture every year.

Every Sunday selected stories and passages that touch on the major themes and seasons of the Christian year are read. The Episcopal Church, for instance, uses a two-year rotating lectionary for the Daily Offices and a three-year cycle of readings for the Eucharist. Other denominations have similar programs.

Sunday readings in the Christmas season, for example, generally concentrate on Jesus' birth and God's judgment. So biblical stories are picked to explore both God's incarnation and his light coming into a dark world. The light of Christ judges the darkness simply by its presence.

THE BOTTOM LINE: Denominational lectionaries can help one choose appropriate biblical stories, as long as they are used discreetly. And there is a bonus: They also act as a connection between what happens in the classroom and what happens in Sunday morning's worship. We shall look at this possibility in the next chapter.

DON'T ATTEMPT TOO MUCH

As helpful as these lectionaries are, however, it is unwise to use a new lesson each week simply because the lectionary calls for it. Indeed, such a method potentially can destroy classroom life.

It is unrealistic to expect to study more than one story in the time allotted to us on a Sunday morning. A few minutes more than thirty are generally all most of us can count on.

Before the term begins, you ought to choose which Bible stories you want to use, and focus, at most, on *one lesson* or story every week or two.

THE BOTTOM LINE: Because experiential education so greatly values student participation in activities like art, song, and drama, the old adage "Less is more" is particularly true when choosing the number of stories to be explored during the term. After all, there is always next year . . . for the rest of our lives.

Choose a few, and enjoy.

TAKE TIME TO EXPLORE

When God and God's people meet, and God's people know it— that is Christian education at its best. Biblical stories are the windows to God's presence and ministry in the world; don't close them before the breeze blows through.

If you and your students like a particular story, be prepared to spend several Sundays with it. Don't be hurried. If information is pushed simply for its own sake or for that of keeping to a schedule, you will lose the children's interest as surely as the sun rises every morning.

THE POINT IS: Generally it is wise to stick with a story until the pupils' interest in it wanes or you have exhausted its possibilities. Class enthusiasm is destroyed by pushing too many stories and too much information at the expense of the imaginative exploration of one interesting story.

I'll bet God is able to use one story, well told and enthusiastically explored, a whole lot better than many stories quickly sketched.

ENHANCING THE COLORADO CURRICULUM

The lectionary-based Colorado Curriculum is rightly favored in Sunday-morning Christian education, and it works even better when joined with *Creative Christian Education.*

The Colorado Curriculum's strength is twofold: (1) its use of Sunday morning's liturgical lections, and (2) its practical help in dealing with biblical stories appropriate to the season. But this strength is also its weakness, for it all too easily trips up the classroom teaching it so ably supports.

The Colorado Curriculum provides a wealth of materials for the Sunday-morning teacher. Three appointed Bible lessons are addressed (only one of which may be an easily told story), along with a psalm and even some prayers. And if that is not a cup running over, just as many new materials are generated for the next week, and the next, and so on.

What of the faithful teachers? To "keep up" with the schedule, they sometimes feel driven to use a new set of lessons every week, and instead of operating under our guidelines of "Less is more," "Success is more" becomes the order of the day. This approach destroys classroom life.

The brief time available for most Sunday-morning educational programs is insufficient to embark on new lessons each week—particularly if they *are* lessons, not stories. If teachers, however, think that is what they ought to be doing to be faithful (which everyone wants to be), it will be done, and their classes will be overwhelmed with a mass of rich materials. I hear this lamentable story over and over again.

Creative Christian Education's use of five seasonal terms provides a happy note of flexibility when used *with* the Colorado Curriculum. Here is how.

Because the seasonal terms carry the theme of parish education, it is acceptable to teach one biblical story for several weeks, even if some classes are using other stories appropriate to the season. The seasonal themes keep all classes current with each other. And because the term-ending parish festivals pull everything together into great big celebrations, everyone will be back in step, again, at six-week intervals.

THE POINT IS: Less is more, given the thirty minutes most of us have in the Sunday-morning classroom. So it is much better to enjoy one story for several weeks than to push ahead just for the sake of "keeping up" with Sunday's worship lectionary. The worship lectionaries of the church are paced for worship; they are not paced for Sunday-morning Christian education. Not to recognize this fact sets teachers up for disappointment.

It is clear: Seasonal terms and themes enhance the Colorado Curriculum.

CLASSROOM ATTENDANCE AND STORYTELLING

The use of biblical stories also helps us with the problems arising from sporadic attendance.

We cannot count anymore on consistent Sunday classroom attendance. Almost everyone's attendance varies, for many reasons. If lesson plans are arranged so that one Sunday's work is built on that of the previous week, more than a bit of trauma will mark class life. Those students who *were* present may soon get bored while you "catch up" the others who were not. Some may begin to misbehave. Then discipline and order become front-burner issues, and all of a sudden, instead of exploring exciting biblical stories, teachers are reduced to managing the class.

POINT: Dramatic stories of people and events are able to stand on their own. If you continue to study a story the following week, it can be quickly retold and explained.

PLANNING TO TEACH

Planning for Sunday's class takes about an hour, maybe a little more, each week. It is greatly simplified if stories fitting a seasonal theme have been preselected.

What about specific plans? In the following excerpt from her (inexpensive and readable) book, Dorothy Furnish takes a look at Moses' leadership of the Hebrew exodus from Egypt (Exodus 1:8 to 15:22) and helps us think through the presentation of a story.

STEP ONE: DISCOVER POSSIBLE EMPHASES AND CHOOSE ONE

Over the years, Bible texts have come to have certain meanings attached to them, but further thought may reveal other implications. To discover the full richness of a passage, follow this plan.

First, read the Bible text and reflect on its importance to you. Do you find parallels in your own life?

Next, read about the passage in a Bible commentary. What have biblical scholars discovered about its authorship, the age in which it was written, the intended audience, and its probable meaning?

Finally, try to imagine what significance children may find in it.

As a result of your study and reflection, select one or more themes that you have discovered are valid in terms of your personal experience, the best of biblical scholarship, and the understanding level of the children.

STEP TWO: DISCOVER POSSIBLE "FEELING-INTO" ACTIVITIES AND CHOOSE ONE

To help children "feel into" the story, it is necessary to identify the feelings of the Bible characters. Ask yourself, "How did the oppressed people in the story feel? Frightened? Angry? Discouraged and resentful?" Then ask, "What activities can children engage in that will help them feel these emotions?" Several possibilities may come to mind.

1. Creative drama—help children imagine themselves as oppressed people.

2. Art—ask children to show through painting and other art forms how it feels to be angry or frightened or discouraged.

3. Discussion—help children recall times when they were angry, frightened, discouraged, or resentful.

STEP THREE: DISCOVER POSSIBLE "MEETING-WITH" ACTIVITIES AND CHOOSE ONE

Ask yourself, "What are some ways the children can 'meet with' the story of Moses that will help them feel they are actually participants in the event?" These are only a few of the possible ways.

1. See a motion picture about Moses.
2. Listen to someone tell the Moses story.
3. Hear a taped dramatization of the story of Moses.

When Bible texts are difficult to "feel into," the "meaning with" must be as exciting and involving as possible. In the Moses account, however, the use of creative drama has such power that a simple, straightforward telling of the story is appropriate.

STEP FOUR: DISCOVER POSSIBLE "RESPONDING-OUT-OF" ACTIVITIES AND CHOOSE ONE

Ask, "In the light of the emphasis I have chosen, and the 'feeling-into' activity I have planned, what response from the children might I expect?" You will want to have several activities in mind, so that you can choose the one most appropriate to the mood of the group.

1. Dance how the story made them feel.
2. Discuss who the oppressed are today.
3. Dramatize the story again.
4. Service project—do something for the oppressed.

The spontaneous response of one group of girls and boys was to dramatize the story again, this time speaking the parts themselves instead of moving in response to the words of a narrator. If you wish to encourage your class members to do this, include it on your planning chart.[1]

Lesson planning may take about an hour or a little more each week. For those of us who like to teach, it is a time of learning and growth. Also it is fun to think of the children and the explorations soon to come.

THE GOOD-NEWS METHOD OF TELLING STORIES

Every chapter in the Bible is a treasure house of good-news stories, each of which has been carefully retold in the hope that the succeeding generations will focus their attention on the good news of God's presence and ministry.

The New Testament word "Gospel" means "good news." The Christian good news is this: God was in Christ, fully identifying himself to the world, showing the world his care, and offering the world a chance to come home to himself.

POINT: Always teach from the perspective of good news, no matter which of the following routines you use.

THE BOTTOM LINE: When good-news biblical stories of God's presence and ministry are shared, enthusiasm and joy abound and Christian education well serves the one for whom we labor. So in every story, look first for the good news of God's presence and ministry, and teach it first.

WARNING: Do not mistake talking "about" good news with exploring a story in such a way that the good news is readily apparent. *Talking* about good news is boring, but *experiencing* the good news of a biblical story is something else again. With just a little bit of experiential education it is easy to do. Do not forget:

I hear and I forget.

I see and I remember.

I do and I understand.

SOME ADDITIONAL HELP: The stories of Bartimaeus receiving his sight and of a lame man cured are grand examples of good news, and some ways and means of telling them and others are described in chapter 11 (the sections *Telling Good News Stories of Jesus* and *The Shape of Good News*). Bible-imaginative speculation lends itself to this endeavor, too.

SIX WAYS TO TELL GREAT STORIES

There are many ways to tell a story. Six of them are listed below, and all are fun. As you read them, remember the Chinese adage:

I hear and I forget.

I see and I remember.

I do and I understand.

A NOTE TO THE SUNDAY-SCHOOL SUPERINTENDENT: learning to use these and other aids ought to be a part of every teacher's training. Procedures for doing so are described in chapter 7.

1. *Mutual Storytelling.* *Mutual storytelling* invites the child to

tell a completely imaginary story to another person, or to write it down, taking as his or her point of departure a story from the Bible. Start with "Daniel was thrown into the lion's den because . . ." and you may get such answers as, "He *loved* God," "He wouldn't give up his *faith*," or "He had a lot of *courage*." Each response is prelude to an exciting and spontaneous story.

A bit later, pick one or several of the principal themes and encourage the children to make up their own imaginary stories. Or put on the blackboard one of the words italicized above, and inquire, "What is *courage*?" In their unique ways, your pupils will learn some of the implications of what it is to be called Christian, and the biblical story of God's presence will find a "home" in their hearts.

2. *Joint Storytelling.* *Joint storytelling* is a method in which the class or individual students "fill in the blanks" as the teacher recounts a story.

> Teacher: I wonder if he were thrown . . .
> Student: Oh, yes. They were mad at him and . . .

There are many ways to involve students in stories, even one as simple as "fill in the ending."

3. *Encouraging Identification.* *Look for feelings* as your pupils identify with their heritage. With just a little help, the children can begin to appreciate their similarity to the persons described in the scriptural stories. Also, sharing your own understanding as you respond to these narratives is a lovely offering; the children will love you for it.

For instance, what color is fear? What color is courage? You may want to have your pupils make a collage based on their responses to these questions.

4. *Raising Questions.* *Ask questions, and wonder* about persons and events. For example:
   a. What was this person like?
   b. Can you describe the event? How would you rewrite the story?
   c. I wonder how she or he felt?
   d. I wonder how I'd (you'd) feel if I (you) were there?

5. *Brainstorming.* *Brainstorming* is another way to involve children in the story. The use of descriptive adjectives, pictures, and colors can also be helpful in fostering an appreciation not only for the events but for the persons involved. These methods tend to stimulate a re-creation of the events, encouraging the pupils' identification with it.

6. *Action/Reflection.* *The action/reflection model* works especially well with adolescents. This style of exploration addresses the students' questions and encourages debate as the questioners struggle to get at the truth of the matter.

Let us illustrate this method with Acts 7, the stoning of Stephen. It is a lesson that, for Episcopalians, always is read a few days after Christmas. The plain fact is, the birth of God's Christ not only meant rejoicing with the shepherds but anger from those who wanted the world to themselves.

First, identify the human situation in the biblical story. What is going on in the lives of the participants? What does the Bible say about God's thoughts and feelings? Do not help the children identify with the story yet; simply concentrate on the story itself.

Second, identify the "sin perspective." How are we abusing God in the story, and how are we abusing one another, ourselves, and creation? The Ten Commandments are a help here. (One of the best brief discussions of them is found in the *Book of Common Prayer,* pages 847 and 848.[2])

Third, look for God's help and resourcefulness. Considering that we are free to create or to destroy, to love or to abuse one another, what is the shape of God's care in the story? The people Stephen met were free to destroy him, and they chose to do so. God made us free. God was not absent from Stephen's death, for, though powerless to stop it (given his respect for human freedom), he was ready to welcome Stephen home. Further, he used Stephen's death to touch the heart of Saul, later to become St. Paul.

To make this model work best, ask these two questions:

—What could God have done differently?

—Why does God value our freedom so much?

The relationship between human freedom and God's self-imposed powerlessness is entailed in the story of Stephen's death. It is a biblical theme of Calvary not much acknowledged today but much on the minds of teenagers and young adults. It is discussed further in chapter 12 (in the section entitled *God's Good Friday—Today*).

THE BENEFIT OF STORYTELLING FOR CHILDREN, TEENS,
AND ADULTS

Lectures are a good way to present information, but they are not the only way—nor, in many cases, are they the best way, for children, teens, or adults.

A better way is storytelling. This is what teachers can expect to happen when biblical stories are imaginatively told:

First, the ever-present natural faith (described in the previous chapter) begins to become Christian. God, who is always near, comes especially near, for in the moment of telling he is named and known. Naming another always makes him or her somehow more present. Because God is named, natural faith—always being formed by God— begins to take the shape of Christian faith.

POINT: When biblical stories are told, an always present God comes especially near and *touches our feelings and stirs our thoughts*.

Faith, whether natural or Christian, has two components—a feeling side and a thoughtful side. It is a combination of both, not simply one or the other. Good teaching honors both as classroom activities are planned.

The feeling side of faith I call "trustful love." It is particularly important when one tells stories to small children, whose faith tends to be characterized by it. In one story we recounted earlier, trustful love in response to God's presence (described in the preceding chapter) took shape at the beach over the course of several years. It also took shape among the six-year-old children at communion, as well as in Lewis Green's classroom.

The thoughtful side of faith I call "reasoned hope." It is particularly important when one tells stories to adolescents and adults. Faith as reasoned hope tends to develop as we mature. For one member of Lewis Green's Sunday-school class, faith as reasoned hope began to form at an early age, though it would not be fully developed for many years. Stephen puts it this way,

I knew I was part of the kingdom in a special way . . . although I would not have named it so at the time.

Because God is experienced as the faithful God he is, we begin to sense there is reason to be hopeful. This is why the study of Scripture is so important for Christians: The Bible paints a bright picture of God's faithfulness in the past, so that the older we get, the more our lives demonstrate, from the perspective of a backward glance informed by Scripture, God's faithful participation.

QUESTION: What does all this mean for the teacher dedicatedly working faithfully away in the Sunday-school classroom? Younger children respond to God with their hearts and feelings. The older we grow, the more we also engage God with our thinking, and faith as reasoned hope develops.

Up through the seventh grade, build your teaching activities around the development of trustful love. Tell Bible stories, act them out, and discuss them with a view to building trustful love, for that is the primary shape of God's ministry.

When teaching adolescents and adults, continue valuing the development of trustful love, but expect reason to generate questions. In particular, encourage teenagers to take issue with scripture's stories of God's action and human life. When honest questions are asked in a community of seasoned faith, God helps us with some answers.

I call this search to understand "St. Thomas's Struggle." The adolescent search to make sense of things—a pilgrimage none of us ever really gives up, always wondering "Why?"—is an expression of our quest for reasoned hope. Support this search, for as children and adults wrestle with scripture's witness and God's presence, both trustful love and reasoned hope combine to build a sturdy faith.

A SEASONED CHRISTIAN FAITH: THE GOAL OF
CHRISTIAN EDUCATION

The older we get, the more trustful love and reasoned hope combine to form what I call seasoned Christian faith. It is a faith emerging from God's presence through the thick and thin of life, a faith rejoicing in the "for better" times of life and deeply aware of God's seeming absence at times of life best characterized as "for worse."

Seasoned Christian faith emerges from the searching-to-make-sense-of-things that characterizes our lives from time to time. Seasoned faith is not only thoughtful, influenced by Scripture and the awareness of God's presence in life, but love refined to an expectant hope that God will always be present, actively doing infinitely more than we can ask for or imagine.

THE BOTTOM LINE FOR SUNDAY-MORNING CHRISTIAN EDUCATION: Age, experience, and reason combine to form a seasoned Christian faith, which is the ultimate goal of every Christian-education program. Further, it is a lifelong journey.

Seasoned faith is to some degree evident in each of the stories cited in the preceding chapter. The sole exception was the story of the six-year-old children wrestling with one another and God at his altar. In it we see the beauty of trustful love. It was not yet time for those youngsters to possess a seasoned Christian faith able to declare that

> Jesus is the only perfect image of the Father, and shows us the nature of God.[3]

Still, by one youngster's referring to Jesus later in the afternoon, we can see the promise and beginnings—even at age six—of seasoned faith. Classroom Christian Education rejoices in such events as these.

CELEBRATE THE STORY WITH DRAMA

Biblical stories offer endless opportunities for acting, and drama is good teaching at its best.

It has been said that we tend to remember something like 30% of what we hear, 40% of what we see, and 80% of what we do.

POINT: For good reason, chancel drama has been used in the life of the Church for centuries: Everyone is involved in the narrative, and in the drama everyone is touched by God.

You may want your children occasionally to be involved in the parish's Sunday-morning worship. I hope you will request it. Parents like it, as do others who see the future of the Church in the promise of its children.

If you see the possibility of a play or skit illuminating Scripture's witness, you may think the idea is yours and only yours. You would, however, be wrong, for God participates in the birth and development of all our ideas. Ideas are the signs of his presence and loving interest. So you have a choice: to honor his ministry by posing the idea you and God are beginning to develop, or deciding not to.

THE BOTTOM LINE: Be prepared to be surprised by the results your seemingly "unusual" ideas may bring.

The person who first proposed the idea of a fire department's Sunday morning visit during the All-Saints term did not realize that adults as well as children would want to look closely at the fire engine and talk to the firemen. Nor did any of us anticipate the parish's excitement at the prospect.

. . . OR MAKE A BANNER

Every biblical story is bright with color and action. Making a colorful banner not only brings the stories home to memory but, like drama, promotes learning at its best. Here is why:

1. Developing a display presupposes that the story is known and understood. The story is studied not because it must be remembered (we do not give tests) but because it is important to the task at hand. God uses tasks like these to write in our minds recollections of his mighty acts done before we were born.

2. Fellowship takes shape as the banner is made. Curiosity and imagination make the classroom a happy and joyful place. Communion develops, not the around-the-altar kind but godly communion nevertheless, and the children are bonded more closely to the Master as surely as the sun also rises.

3. When the banners are displayed, recognition and outright affection will be the parish's responses. Children blossom in such a responsive atmosphere. And because it is God's ministry we are celebrating, parish life is considerably enhanced.

On presentation day the banners can be processed with the choir and the clergy and recognized during announcements. Perhaps class members will offer carefully prepared explanations of them. Later the banners can be hung in the church, the parish hall, or some other prominent place for a while. Banners ought to be displayed in the *most* prominent places. Here is Christian education at its best.

A PLACE FOR MEMORIZATION AND RECITATION

Memorization is appropriate for pupils of all ages, although we educators don't seem to value it nearly as much as we once did. But I have learned otherwise.

On more than a few occasions I have stood by the bedside of the dying, offering prayers or readings from Scripture, as requested or as I have suggested. Many are the times I have found their lips moving

along with mine as we read the Beautitudes or shared the Lord's
Prayer. It seems everyone knows "In My Father's House Are Many
Mansions" (John 14:2) and the Twenty-third Psalm. Sometimes a
peaceful smile forms on the reciter's lips, at other times tears, the
gentle, eye-filling kind, flow.

Several people later recollected all sorts of memories that emerged
in those moments—times early in life when God met them through
parents, friends, or Church-school teachers, warm memories of life
when it seemed full, but a life held even yet, as then, in the everlasting
arms of one always with us (Deuteronomy 33:27).

We owe it to our children to offer this kind of preparation for their
future. I have worked with a congregation during the season of Lent,
learning with them the Twenty-third Psalm, and I have had people
thank me for it afterward. At such times the community of faith was
joined in a common educational endeavor, and communion took place
in our midst.

I am not suggesting memorization as mere "busy work," or that it
ever be pushed as a task to be harshly evaluated. But briefly engaged
in week after week in the classroom and in Sunday's worship, occasional memorization will, I believe, provide reference points around
which we can all the more easily be engaged by the presence of God
as one known to us in our midst.

We all die. When that final hour approaches, I hope we, too, will
be able, through verse, hymn, and prayer, to join with the wider
communion of saints, remembering times when we were touched not
only by others but by Another.

The Sunday-school class offers us more than we shall ever know.

ENTHUSIASM AND RAPTURE

The word "enthusiasm" is rooted in the Greek *en* (in) and *theos*
(God). When we are in God, we are enthusiastic people, and that is
what your Sunday-school will be like when you tell stories the experiential way.

When we draw pictures in the classroom, memorize and read
aloud together, act out stories, sing and maybe dance, happy enthusiasm is a sign of the presence of God. We can count on it. We become
wrapped up in God's spirit. The word "rapture" does not occur in
the Bible, but it is an ancient expression of what it is like when we
are touched by God's always-near presence. At such times—and they

may last for no more than a few seconds—we feel joyful and peaceful. Tears may signal these events, the gently rolling kind, or we may end up taking a big breath, trying to keep things under control.

Rapture cannot be willed, though we can expect and indeed plan for it. Rapture is precisely what we can expect to feel and witness when biblical stories are well taught.

Have fun and enjoy.

Notes

1. Dorothy Jean Furnish, *Living the Bible with Children* (Nashville: Abingdon Press, 1979), 87–103. [Note: Her book *Exploring the Bible with Children* (1975) is also helpful, though the materials in the two works overlap.]

2. *The Book of Common Prayer*, 1979.

3. Ibid., 849.

CHAPTER SIX

Parish Worship— A Means of Grace

GOD MEETS US WHERE WE ARE

God's presence is especially potent when the Church gathers for worship.

> Isaiah was at worship. It was probably a festival occasion, and the music was grand.
>
> But of all those present, he alone saw the Lord sitting upon a throne,
>
> ". . . High and lifted up, and his train filled the temple" (Isaiah 6:1).
>
> In the midst of bright colors, chanting voices and the sweet smell of burning incense, the Word of God took articulate shape in color, smell, and volume, and the course of Isaiah's life was changed forever.

Those who served with God in the development of that day's worship would have made first-rate, contemporary Christian educators.

And here is a mystery: When worship's prayers, music, and pageantry combine, God's word becomes an especially vital presence and our lives are changed.

WORSHIP AND FALLING IN LOVE WITH GOD

Though it might not be as cataclysmic as Isaiah's, at the root of religion there is always the experience of the holy.

Love is first generated by an awareness touching our hearts, and liturgical worship provides a place for it to happen—not the only place but an expected and important place.

Priscilla describes her early experience in Sunday worship this way:

> As a small child I attended a nearby Methodist Church with my parents and sister. Sundays were always special. We had doughnuts or coffee cake for breakfast. I often got to wear my very favorite pink dress, my straw hat with a blue ribbon and, best of all, my shiny "maryjane" patent leather shoes with black bows.
>
> I loved racing my sister up the steps of the church to the big double doors. The people at the door were always warm and friendly and gave me a "folder." It had a lot of words on the inside that I didn't really understand. But no matter, what I liked best about the folder was the picture on the front. Sometimes there were flowers or churches, but the ones I like best had a picture of Jesus, sometimes one of Jesus with little children.
>
> Being little myself, I felt that Jesus was sort of saying, "These big people are important here, but I really love being with little children like you." I felt warm inside.
>
> Then my parents would take me to the nursery while they went to the "big" church. That was a time I kind of wished I were bigger.
>
> While the nursery was fun, I could hardly wait to be old enough to go with them. The church always looked lovely. It had a bright red rug and a "table" with a white cloth, a cross, and lovely flowers.
>
> And that moment came much sooner than I expected.
>
> One Christmas we children were asked to dramatize the nativity scene. On Christmas Eve! Some were picked to be shepherds or the wise men. I waited, and jumped for joy as the teacher asked me to play the part of Mary.
>
> I don't really remember the rehearsals, but that Christmas Eve—in the "big" church with candles and beautiful music—was the most exciting time in my young life.
>
> As I sat there with a blue shawl over my head and a doll baby in my arms, Christmas carols rang so clearly I still remember the sound. My favorite picture was really true. Jesus really did love little children. And he loved me! I felt special, prized, unique and wrapped in a warm glow of love. And I remember that time to this day.

God bonds us to himself, and worship is his mighty instrument. It is a means of grace. Christian education simply cannot afford to exclude parish worship from its program, for the plain truth is:

I hear and I forget.

I see and I remember.

I do and I understand.

SUNDAY WORSHIP AND THE CLASSROOM

I once helped a couple—Jenny and Frank Wright—celebrate their sixtieth wedding anniversary during a Sunday morning's worship. Over several months in the All-Saints term, we made careful preparations for the celebration. Every Sunday-school class was involved. A zoo, you say? It required careful administration, but that, too, is an important part of Sunday-morning Christian education.

The classes explored modern marriage and family life. In some cases, the children interviewed their mothers and fathers. They brought to class photographs of their parents' weddings. For the children of single parents, this was an opportunity to find out what it had been like "once upon a time," something we had not anticipated.

One class made a big, bright banner highlighting some milestones in the Wrights' life—for example, their births and marriage, the purchase of their home, the births of their children. Because Frank had once worked for the United States Postal Service, the town's Post Office was also pictured. That banner still hangs in the parish hall, reminding the parishioners of the Wrights' happy memories.

The big Sunday finally came, and our worship celebrated not only Frank and Jenny's sixtieth anniversary but every marriage in the parish. The church was packed with friends, many of whom came for the first time. It was a day of remembering and celebration, and it was glorious.

> Later, a 37-year-old member of St. Andrew's who'd known the Wrights all her life said she'd cried a bit during the service, but "I never felt closer to them or to myself than today. I wish church were like this more often."[1]

Though this anonymous commentator makes no mention of God, it was God's presence she felt. Further, Frank and Jenny's smiles radiated God's glory and just hinted at the congregation's joy.

You may say, if you want, that these are just expressions of human feelings and that all we had was a good time. But you would be wrong,

THE Episcopalian

FEBRUARY, 1977

TRADITIONAL SCOTTISH MUSIC and atmosphere heralded Jenny and Frank Wright's 60th wedding anniversary celebration at St. Andrew's.

Parish celebrates an anniversary

"How can a parish celebrate 60 years of marriage?" was the question the Rev. Howard Hanchey asked his staff at St. Andrew's, Meriden, Conn.

The idea sprang from a casual conversation one morning with parishioner Frank Wright, born in Scotland 87 years ago, who mentioned prayers that were offered on his and his wife's 50th anniversary. "Frank's comment that there were only three of the original wedding party left alive caught my attention," Hanchey says. "Sixty years deserves recognition and more than a few prayers, and I wanted to provide them it we could."

After a number of conversations with the Wrights and other parishioners, the liturgy began to take shape. Explaining it to the parish Hanchey said, "Frank and Jenny offer to St. Andrew's a profound moment, and I invite you to join in an engagement, for perhaps an hour, with yourselves, those around you, your spouses and children, and perhaps discern a bit more fully the hand of God at work among the people of His world."

Both the congregation and the larger Meriden community joined one Sunday morning in the celebration of the mar-riage. With a contemporary setting and some traditional Scottish music, more than 350 persons joined to pay tribute. The service included a reaffirmation of vows not only for the Wrights, but for all wedded members of the congregation.

The Sphinx Temple Highlanders pipers, of which Wright serves as chaplain and piper, provided some of the liturgy's music; the presentation hymn at the offertory was "Amazing Grace."

In the church school children spent several classroom hours exploring marriage in general. After the service they held a reception for the Wrights and presented them with a liturgical banner depicting their 60 years of marriage. "We used Frank and Jenny, in a way, with their permission," says Hanchey, "but with marriage and family life coming under such current pressure, our worship and its preparation were good teaching vehicles."

Later a 37-year-old member of St. Andrew's who'd known the Wrights all her life said she'd cried a bit during the service, but "I never felt closer to them or to myself than today. I wish church were like this more often."

for God was at work in the midst of things, just as he always is, and his ministry is that of celebrating life—our lives and his.

THE BOTTOM LINE IS: Worship is an event through which God announces his presence and sharpens our knowledge of it. So it was for Isaiah, and so it was for the young woman quoted above, and so it is for us.

Christian education is impoverished when it is unrelated to Sunday's worship. When, however, the connection is made, true education takes place.

BUILDING A CATHEDRAL

Everybody likes a celebration. Just as families look forward to summer vacations, so do Christian parishioners look forward to term-ending celebrations. Every festival is anticipated for at least six weeks. If you count the rest of the year and the anticipation latent in class explorations during the other terms, the preparations are even more extensive. Granted, planning is not always done consciously, but group thought and the unconscious cannot be overlooked.

As the weeks fly by, an atmosphere of parish camaraderie develops. A cathedral is built, not from stone and mortar but from collective anticipation. Specific plans gradually emerge, not because they have to but because the process moves naturally in their direction.

The Epiphany term, for example, lends itself to explorations of such topics as children and communion, parish life and ministry, baptism and confirmation. On one occasion an Episcopal parish's two-hundred-member adult class became a confirmation class for everyone, those confirmed and those not. For six weeks everyone explored the heritage of their denomination. The Eucharists and Daily Offices preceding the Sunday-school classes were often instructed, not every Sunday but more often than not, and sermons were preached with this study in mind.

At the term's concluding festival the church was filled for the bishop's visitation, sixty children and adults were baptized and confirmed, and it all happened in only eighty minutes.

The All-Saints festival lends itself to a great procession of antique and modern saints. With careful planning and direction and a printed schedule of worship, the service need not be inordinately extended.

The Christmas festival can be built around the pageant with attendant carols, and Palm Sunday lends itself to a dramatic congregational reading of the Passion Gospel. Some parishes even borrow a donkey for the day.

Music can be nicely enhanced by a trumpet and maybe even timpani and strings. Use your imagination; it is one of the best of God's gifts.

What can we expect of God's ministry at such times? An eighty-year-old parishioner put it this way, with a twinkle in her eye:

> You know, these children aren't learning what I learned in Sunday school. All I remember is that I didn't like it.

My mind boggles at how old, unpleasant experiences can damage the adult's potential for learning. Conversely, in the life of one older Christian, God redeemed a memory and made things new at eighty. God is good.

STANDING ROOM ONLY

Christians' heightened sense of anticipation at Christmas and Easter tells the above story, too. At these times most churches are packed. Though more than a few of us tend to ridicule those who "show up" only for these holidays, they seem to be remembering "old times" when they were fed with a bread that endures. They have returned to church, looking for it again.

On these holidays the worship of the Church thrives as at few other times. Generally it is because of well-laid plans, powerful music, and group participation of such a caliber that it outdoes "the greatest show on earth." Isaiah would know this is true.

This chapter's BOTTOM LINE: Term-ending festivals encourage the open atmosphere that experiential education requires. They bring everything together by providing study goals and promising celebration. By getting your classes to prepare for them, you will have every reason to expect "standing room only," just as at Christmas and Easter.

THROW A PARTY

Cancel classes on festival Sundays, and in their place provide a reception for the parish community. The atmosphere generated by God in worship will continue in the more informal parish-hall setting.

These occasions also enable God's people to begin to know one another. Name tags ought to be used.

AND THERE IS A BONUS: These festivals provide the teaching personnel with a Sunday break, and, while putting a joyful end to one term (and its theme), provide a clear point of departure for the next.

WELCOMING VISITORS

During festivals people will be present who are not regularly a part of parish life. They may be interested friends or neighbors, or grandparents, aunts, uncles, or cousins. Potentially they can get lost in the celebration. So, with all these additional folks and a "standing room only" congregation, it makes sense to print and distribute the schedule of worship, including the texts of the hymns, lessons, and prayers. It is hard to read from several books, no matter how familiar they may be, and it is especially difficult in an unfamiliar service.

Although it creates extra work for the office staff, providing printed explanations is especially helpful when many persons are involved in complex coordination. Using both sides of 8½-inch by 14-inch sheets of paper allows one to print an eight-page schedule on four sheets.

THE BOTTOM LINE: A mimeographed schedule of worship, complete with every hymn, prayer, and reading, along with carefully written explanations provides for easy dispatch, without confusion and hurry. Such aids are often provided at Christmas and Easter, and God's ministry is nicely served by like care during the other term-ending festivals.

The flexibility to accommodate these festivals is provided, for Episcopalians, in the Order for Celebrating the Holy Eucharist, on page 400 of the *Book of Common Prayer*. The careful preparations required proceed naturally from each term's topics.

THE CHURCH LOSES—WHEN CHILDREN ARE LEFT OUT

Stanley Smith conducted an interesting study of growth patterns in Australian Churches from 1963 to 1975. He found that in that twelve-year period membership in Roman Catholic, Lutheran, and Mormon churches increased, whereas Episcopal, Presbyterian, and Methodist churches showed declines.

Smith found only one common denominator. When children were

separated from the communal worship and sent to another place, membership in those churches declined. Growing churches, Smith found, expected children to take part in worship, and they provided accordingly for the latter's participation. Declining churches "hid children away."

My own informal research confirms Smith's findings.

THE BOTTOM LINE: In churches where Christian education flourishes, *careful provision* is made to welcome children into Sunday morning's worship. The memberships of those same churches are growing more rapidly than the general population.

Smith comments,

> I am not preaching a Gospel of children, but I question whether the Gospel can be heard in congregations that refuse to allow children's presence. One trend which is particularly destructive and demoralizing to children is the practice of having Sunday school groups meeting at the same time as the main worship service. Constantly dividing up the church on the basis of age and sex copies a worldly, high-school model of education.[2]

Parish worship is a means of graceful education, designed by God for both young and old. It is a special device for nurture and conversion. Priscilla, quoted earlier, made exactly this point in her story.

CHILDREN, GOD'S GRACE, AND COMMUNION

God's Holy Communion is a means of grace, and God uses it as a profound educational device. In it natural faith is strengthened, and because of it natural faith begins to become Christian.

The discussions of faith in chapter 4 (beginning with *The Birth of Faith* and particularly in *Christian Faith's Growth in the Classroom*) and chapter 5 (*The Benefit of Storytelling for Children, Teens, and Adults*) both point in the direction of joining young children with the Eucharist. If you want to bring up children in the Christian faith, you must not shackle this means of grace. All too often we treat God's Holy Communion as belonging more to us than to God. (By "us" I mean adult Christians.) Those who limit children's participation in the Eucharist are on the wrong track. By limiting the participation of children in the Eucharist, we are not being the faithful servants God expects.

The word "education" is rooted in the Latin *educere*, meaning "to lead forth" or "to bring up." Fundamentally, God uses communion "to lead [us] forth" into relationship with him, and "to bring [us] up" into an ever-greater trust in his faithfulness. It is powerful education, not the "book-learning" kind but that which God seems to enjoy best.

POINT: God's Holy Communion is the feeding of every new person in Christ, for just as meals at home provide for our physical, spiritual, and emotional health, so, too, does communion at the Lord's table in church. Particularly for the very young, from newborns on, in God's Holy Communion Christian faith is born and strengthened. Every story in chapter 4 shows the effects of God's presence in our lives.

IT ALL BEGINS WITH BAPTISM

Baptism symbolizes a Christian's birth into the Church family. Once born, we need to be fed, but in most denominations, only adults are admitted to the Lord's table. Adult baptism (or confirmation, for those baptized as infants) is a prerequisite. The assumption is that instruction and knowledge are necessary *before* we approach the Lord's table. If family life at home, however, were based on the same assumption, none of us would be around to grow up.

Think for just a moment about what it is like to be fed as a Christian. Learning biblical stories is one kind of feeding, and prayer is another. But there is still another way God helps us grow up, though it is all too often closed to young children: He feeds us in the breaking of the bread.

Here is a mystery, deepened by this surprising fact: We human beings learn *before* we are born! Apparently the brain is not switched on at birth, nor even a few days or months after birth; with it we begin learning while being formed in the womb. Author Muriel Beadle writes:

> The psychologists Jack Bernard and Lester W. Sontag once tested fetal response to sound by placing a loudspeaker close to the mother's abdomen (but not in contact with it, to assure that sound waves would travel through air).
>
> They found that the broadcast sound caused the rate of fetal heartbeat to increase sharply. This didn't prove, of course, that the unborn was hearing—only that it was sensitive to sound stimulus.
>
> Something a little more ambitious was then attempted by David K. Spelt (who, like Jack Bernard and a number of other psy-

chologists mentioned in these pages, started out in academic life but shifted to consultive work for business).

Spelt's experiment was to use sound in "conditioning" unborn babies; that is, he decided that he would try to teach them to transfer to stimulus B a response originally elicited by stimulus A.

Spelt's version of this kind of experiment began by securing the cooperation of sixteen pregnant women who were past the seventh calendar month of gestation.

He divided them into several groups. With one group, he ascertained that a vibrator applied to a maternal abdomen would not disturb the fetus sufficiently to cause movement. Experience with another group showed that a loud noise just outside the mother's body (an oak clapper hitting a pine box) *would* cause fetal movement. Then, using a third group, Spelt combined the vibrator and the sound—timing them so that there was a few seconds' lag after he started the vibrator and before he loosed the clapper.

After 15–20 pairings of the vibrator-plus-sound, the fetuses began to move in response to the vibrator alone. In two cases, the experiment was interrupted for more than two weeks, yet when the expectant mothers returned to Spelt's laboratory, their unborn babies "remembered" the experience and again moved in response to the vibrator alone.

Such experiments are not as bizarre as they might at first seem to a layman.

Birth is really only one point in developmental time, one event in a continuum of existence—the beginning of which has a special aura of mystery because it is hidden.[3]

It is hard to say if we are ever too young to learn, and harder still to describe God's participation in our learning processes, but the facts are, we *do* learn and God *does* participate. God's Holy Communion for the young child is a powerful educational medium.

As children share the table with parents and friends, like their parents they, too, are fed by God.

Natural faith is born and slowly becomes Christian as the act of communion is interpreted by the words "This is my body" and "This is my blood."

In the last decade most Christian denominations have begun to own up to the fact that few adults, if any, deeply understand the mystery and power of Holy Communion; at best they only scratch the surface. We also have begun to see that God uses his table to meet us where we are, no matter what our age.

The practice of separating baptism and communion originated

after the early Church became the official Church of the Roman Empire. As Church memberships swelled, the bishops were no longer able to baptize everyone who requested it, so they instructed their priests to conduct the ceremony and then, when convenient, to present the newly baptized persons to them so the rite could be confirmed.

Centuries later, because confirmations were scheduled more infrequently (again because of Church growth), it seemed necessary to withhold communion until after confirmation, to make sure God's people would present themselves for confirmation. For this discipline we can thank the twelfth century's Bishop Peckham.[4]

Today we put birth and feeding more closely together, just as they are in family life and just as they were in the early Church. No baptized person ought to be denied feeding once he or she is born into the Christian family.

THE BOTTOM LINE: Gently, over the course of many Sundays and throughout the pupils' early years, natural curiosity, the mystery of the Eucharist, and God's action at the table combine to form the children into Christians. This is profound education.

We more than flirt with "works righteousness"—the notion that knowledge or action wins us God's favor and makes us presentable to him—when we delay first communion until a time of understanding or belief. Precommunion preparation, unfortunately, conveys the message that, to be fed by God at his table, baptized persons must know "more" than they do. God is not well served thereby.

Depending on God's ministry and the educational power of table fellowship, how, then, do we best serve Sunday-school pupils?

From the outset, children ought to share the Lord's table with their families or other sponsors, for then they will be especially engaged by God. Therefore, instead of holding "communion classes" for children so they can "understand better," involve them in communion from the beginning. Let God explain things in their hearts, and then, as their questions emerge, engage them in rational discourse.

Here the participation of parents or other sponsors is a too-seldom-used asset, for mealtime prayers at home are the logical forerunners of enlightening discussions (see the section *Making the Most of Christian Worship at Home,* below).

Childhood curiosity and imagination then combine with God's action to engender Christian faith. Why can we draw this conclusion? Because I have heard more than one small child say, "Jesus," as the host was offered.

That is God's mighty act. We can depend on it.

INCLUDING CHILDREN:
THE SERMON AND THE CHILDREN'S HOMILY

Forcing very young children to sit through lengthy sermons is abusive. If they are going to participate in worship on Sunday morning, considerate plans must be made for them. Suggestions follow. Each has been used, and each works. All share a common denominator—they keep families together for communion by offering options for children in lieu of the sermon.

Some congregations are finding a bright, brief homily before or after the lessons to be just right. Adults listen closely to it, too. Youngsters, gathered in a small community at an appropriate place, end up feeling prized as the special people they are—to God and to us. This, in my opinion, is good education.

When a homily for children is offered in conjunction with the lessons, the sermon can be preached at the end of the morning's worship. By that time the children will have been released to the classroom. Adults and older children should remain for the sermon, which they are physically and emotionally better equipped to sit through.

But what if you want children of all ages to participate in the Table Liturgy? Some congregations move the sermon to a time following communion. The children join their parents in worship right from the opening hymn, share communion with their families, and leave after they have been fed. Later the adults can focus their attention on the preached word, free from the natural restlessness of children.

Still other churches provide a children's chapel for use during the sermon. The worship is tailored to children's needs. Then the children join the rest of the community for the Peace, and communion includes everyone. Each Sunday morning, this plan offers children the option to listen to the sermon or not; the children's attitudes toward it will, of course, vary from week to week.

Yet another parish does it this way: Gathering as a congregation of families, couples, and singles, everyone joins in a grandly sung opening hymn. Announcements follow, and then the children are released to their classrooms or a children's chapel. The sermon is preached, and when the Sunday-school classes return to worship for the Peace, the children know exactly where their parents are sitting and can go straight to them.

THE BOTTOM LINE IS: If children are to be included, it is necessary to plan the Sunday-morning worship with the *whole* parish in mind.

Still, setting children apart for their own worship and classes means some adults will inevitably miss the sermon. That is a draw-back. All these approaches, no matter how well intended, discourage some teachers, and you may as well expect some chronic but legiti-mate complaints.

Yet there is hope. The use of team teaching helps considerably, for it means that those who do not want to teach for a full year don't have to. (Team teaching is discussed in the next chapter.)

It takes work to construct a satisfactory Sunday-morning schedule that fits the needs and hopes of as few as twenty or as many as three thousand people, ranging in age from a few weeks to a hundred years.

INCLUDING CHILDREN: DISCIPLINE IN PARISH WORSHIP

It is unrealistic to expect everyone automatically to "know" what constitutes good behavior in worship; what might be okay to one family may well be intrusive to another.

A few guidelines and general understandings go a long way in helping a parish tolerate its natural diversity. They also make the participation of children in worship more a joy than a lonely, parent-centered hassle.

Children are children, persons in the process of being socialized to the needs of community. So, you ask, what help is there?

Educational psychologists say there is a marked drop in any group's attention after the first twenty minutes of organized activity; its members' thoughts tend to "wander," and boredom sets in, bore-dom being just another expression of mild anger, like feet swinging and nail chewing. Liturgical planning needs to take account of this limitation.

The same psychologists also say that the group's interest rises following a break. If we are going to encourage families to participate in parish worship, we need to take attention spans into account, too.

I am *not* suggesting, however, that we construct the worship around the "least common denominator"; we adults need to be able to enjoy a worship that meets us where we are.

Children can rise to the occasion with good behavior. It was true for us as we grew up, and it is just as true for them today. All they need is a little guidance—primarily from their parents but from every-one else as well.

Here is a three-step plan that works:

1. Parents and other adults need to agree on *a few realistic guidelines* for children of all ages.

2. These *guidelines must be published and distributed throughout the parish* and regularly explained. They should describe a style of consistent parenting (not nagging), the entire adult community exercising a caring responsibility for the children.

But, you object, suppose "little Jeanne" begins to raise a ruckus during the lesson and Mom and Dad seem to be having trouble with her; what do you do then? When little Jeanne turns around to you, your best bet is not to reward her with a smile but to shake your head, frowning. God loves us as we are, but he expects us to learn to honor the life of people in community. At that moment you will be God's word for Jeanne.

Dan remembers discipline this way:

> I once sat on the back pew in church and played a game of marbles with my friend. We were absolutely sure no one could hear, but we were only deceiving ourselves.
>
> It was during the sermon, and with a start both of us suddenly realized a silence where a short while before there'd been a drone. The preacher had stopped! And everyone was turned around looking at us. I'll never forget it.
>
> Not another word was said for the longest kind of time—though really it wasn't more than a minute. But it was the longest minute I ever spent.
>
> What did I learn? I learned my actions mattered, and that worship and the sermon mattered as well.
>
> The preacher never said a word to me about what happened. And I'm glad he didn't. He knew I knew. And I've never forgotten it.

Children can quietly color a picture or simply sit still. It is a surprise to some parents that their children can, indeed, respect the needs of older persons. This same respect takes shape in living and dining rooms at home.

To help us include children in the Eucharist, a portion of the action of the Peace may be designated as "wiggle time." The Peace, when placed at the time of the offertory, functionally becomes a time not only to respond to one another but to allow for children's enthusiasms, questions, and some appropriate "acting out."

By occasionally pointing out the community's needs in worship, an atmosphere of mutual respect and toleration is created.

3. Of course, it is important to *provide a crib nursery* for the very young.

FIVE RULES FOR GOOD CONDUCT IN THE CHURCH COMMUNITY

Here is a set of behavioral guidelines drawn up by one parish. It worked there (your needs may well be different). THE POINT IS: Children and adults need to live within boundaries commonly understood, agreed on, and actively supported by everyone.

1. Be on time for church school class and worship: 9:30 A.M. and 10:30 A.M.,
   > because
   things are better begun together.
2. Do not run or scream in the halls or in the church building itself
   > because
   attention is fragile, and community life on Sunday morning needs to be carefully cultivated.
3. Go to the bathroom:
   —before church school begins,
   —in the fifteen minutes between classroom activity, and
   —at the beginning of worship in church or
   —after church,
   > because
   personal needs, when community life is involved, must account to elementary discipline.
4. If one really must leave during worship, do so only between readings of the lessons, or hymns, or at the time of the Peace
   > because
   the attention of the community at worship is drawn from its task to the person in transit.
5. If you are late for worship, enter in the periods between the lessons or during hymns:
   —not during readings,
   —nor the sermon,
   —never during the prayers,
   —nor during the choir anthem.
   > because
   The attention of a worshiping community is easily broken:
   —those listening have made a commitment to hear,
   —those reading have made a commitment to speak,

—those preaching have made a commitment to the Bible's word
   and God's people,
—those singing have made a commitment to rejoice.

MAKING THE MOST OF CHRISTIAN WORSHIP AT HOME

Though Sunday-morning Christian education is this book's focus,
I realize God also meets us in our family life at home; education takes
place there as well.

We live in a fractured world. Family life is often complex, and
personal schedules on more than a few occasions clash. Mothers and
fathers scatter to various workplaces. The children, when not in the
school classroom, are engaged in a multitude of extracurricular activities.

Each of us has a daily journey, from the time we get up in the
morning until the time we lay our heads down at night (if we work
the day shift, that is), and each of us covers terrain different from that
of every other member of the family. God has been with us, and he
knows where we have been. Though we may not have been with one
another during the day, we are joined with each other in him.

Christian worship at home may take the form of bedtime prayers,
grace at meals, or scheduled Bible readings. Religion is, by definition,
a discipline, and almost every Christian family has worked out a dis-
ciplined way to remember God's sovereignty and offer thanks to him
daily.

I suggest, however, that family prayer be held at the evening meal.
This approach has proved helpful to more than a few parishioners,
though most have tailored it to their families' particular schedules.

Usually when we sit down to table there is a time of perfunctory
prayer. It often initiates the more important act of eating. But things
don't have to be this way.

We come to dinner hungry. Why not briefly give thanks to God,
as we often do at other times, and without feeling bad about such a
short prayer, begin to enjoy the food and company he provides?

But here is a new twist to an old scenario: Carefully attend to
more than the food, paying particularly close attention to conversation
about the events of the day. You will find that interest, questions, and
a willingness to share experiences mark such a meal's conversation.
(No one, however, ought to be forced to share, particularly reticent
teenagers.)

As parents model this kind of sharing and careful listening, and as children are encouraged to share their day's journey, the family itself begins to get a sense of its immediate history, both for better and for worse (I assume the day will have held disappointment for some). The family members begin to know one another a bit more fully. As the mealtime draws to a close, someone (designated beforehand) might ask that eyes be closed, offering to God the events of the day, perhaps with a bit of Bible-imaginative speculation. Others can be encouraged to "chime in" with their own ideas and feelings.

Cathedral bells won't sound any better to God's ears.

There are other times during the day when the family story can be told and celebrated, but I don't know of a much more convenient one for most of us than mealtime. With just a smidgen of parental guidance, these conversations can be a grand moment for children to deepen their understanding of God's presence in the Eucharist. Christian education is thereby moved out of Sunday only and into the life of the home.

Worship is truly a means of grace; through it God comes especially near, in church on Sunday or at home.

Notes

1. "Parish Celebrates an Anniversary," *The Episcopalian* (February 1977).

2. "Keep Kids Out, Lose Members?" *The Virginia Churchman* (November 1979), 7.

3. Muriel Beadle, *A Child's Mind* (New York: Jason Aronson, 1974), 3–5. Beadle cites several studies on the way human beings learn before birth. Data like hers encourage an appreciation for our early readiness to meet God and to respond to his first overtures.

4. Charles P. Price and Louis Weil, *Liturgy for Living* (New York: The Seabury Press, 1979), 120. The authors provide a historical review of confirmation's relationship to communion, and they cite Peckham's discipline.

CHAPTER SEVEN

September Start-Up: The Practical Details

FIVE ESSENTIALS FOR SUNDAY-MORNING SUCCESS

Setting up a church school brings together five components, each of which is essential for success. Four of them—clergy interest, teacher enthusiasm, clearly defined tools, and parental support—were detailed in this book's opening chapters. The important task of enlisting parental and parish support is picked up in this chapter, and added is the invitation to students.

TEACHER ENTHUSIASM

Teacher enthusiasm is always crucial, so I shall note it again, this time from a slightly different perspective.

Potential teachers are often afraid of failure, and that fear puts a great big damper on their enthusiasm. That is why the previous chapters have carefully detailed some of the ways and means of teaching and have stressed God's fundamental ministry in the enterprise; such knowledge helps ensure success.

Teacher enthusiasm is surely a necessity. Students are "turned on" by teachers who care and can show it and with whom God's presence and ministry are more than a mere lesson.

Bruce writes this way about one important teacher:

> I don't recall any particular moment in my early Christian education that stands out as unique. Nor do I recall any distinctive topic or lesson that had a sudden, powerful impact on me.

What I do recall are special teachers—teachers who, through their brief relationship with me, made lasting impressions. Perhaps the most prominent is Mrs. Cobb. She taught my fourth grade class.

My relationship with Mrs. Cobb marked an important time of transition in my life. My family had just moved into town. I was being resocialized in a new community. That can be tough work for a fourth grader.

What I recall about being in Mrs. Cobb's class is more an emotional memory than anything else. With Mrs. Cobb I felt free to totally be myself, confident that she would like me just as I was. I did not have to win her favor nor did I have to fear losing it. Mrs. Cobb cared, and it showed.

Like any fourth grader, more often than I like to remember I listened more to myself and my friends than to Mrs. Cobb. But no matter, I always felt secure in that special relationship because I "sensed" that her favor transcended both of us. What I learned was this: I am valuable, and I deserve to be valued despite myself.

Since then I've come to realize I was not alone in that classroom with Mrs. Cobb and my friends.

God was present too, valuing me and bonding me into a relationship with him stronger every year, though I would never have said so then.

God touched this young man's life through Mrs. Cobb. Unfortunately, like many teachers, Mrs. Cobb may never know the value of her presence or the shape of God's ministry in those moments along the way. Thanks to Bruce, we, however, can see it all plainly: Mrs. Cobb did not fail, though she may never know the full measure of her success. In her faithful steps we follow.

PARENTAL SUPPORT AND AN INVITATION TO STUDENTS

Parental support and an invitation to students are the last two of the five essential components.

How many students will there be, and where will the teachers come from? These are very important questions. Happily, they are easy to answer, by using just two simple tools—preregistration in the spring and registration in the fall.

PREREGISTRATION IN THE SPRING

Preregistration in the spring is best. A model registration form, one that also doubles as a class roll follows.

CLASS ROLE

All Saints

Sept. ____	Oct. ____
Sept. ____	Oct. ____
Oct. ____	Oct. ____

Festival Eucharist

Nov.____

Christmas

Nov. ____	Nov. ____
Nov. ____	Dec. ____
Nov. ____	Dec. ____

Festival Eucharist

Dec.____

Epiphany

Jan. ____	Feb. ____
Jan. ____	Feb. ____
Jan. ____	Feb. ____
Jan. ____	Feb. ____

Festival Eucharist

Feb.____

Lent

March ____	March____
March ____	April ____
March ____	April ____

Festival Eucharist

April____

Easter/Pentecost

April ____	May ____
May ____	May ____
May ____	May ____

Festival Eucharist

June____

CHURCH SCHOOL FAMILY REGISTRATION FORM

Parish Christian education is a whole parish affair. It includes every one of the entire parish family, and every family, no matter its make-up, can help our enterprize by completing this form and turning it in by registration day. We'll duplicate as necessary and, thanks, too, for acknowledging your part in this year's endeavor.

Student's names: **Age:**   **Grade:**

_____   _____   _____

_____   _____   _____

_____   _____   _____

_____   _____   _____

_____   _____   _____

Parent or Guardian:
Mr. and/or Mrs. _____

Address _____

Telephone_____

The instruction and guidance given to our children by their church school teachers is a gift of love. Please respond below with your contribution — understanding that in these days of inflation there is little that has any real value **except** our **time**. Please be as specific as possible . . . e.g. I sew, or embroider, or paint, or cook, or bake bread, or like to garden, or carpenter, or mold clay, or do funny line drawings, or read well, or tell stories, or have dramatic ability, etc. Don't belittle any gift you have, and might be willing to share.

Yes, I will give some time__, and my hobbies and talents are:

List them without judging their value to our parish family. We will be in your debt if you will leave us free to evaluate their usefulness, as we survey classroom needs.

I will fulfill my responsibility as an adult Christian by:

(check one)   assisting _____ observing _____

in the _____ grade class during the _____ term.

Set aside several weeks toward the close of the Easter/Pentecost term, and concentrate the parishioners' attention on the needs of, and the opportunities for, next year's program.

What does preregistration accomplish? First, it begins to build an atmosphere of anticipation and expectation, for the spring is thereby linked to the next autumn. Continuity is emphasized and anticipation fostered.

Second, early estimates of the size and number of classes can be made. Teacher interest is stimulated, and the task of enlisting teachers is, therefore, made all the easier. God is at work here, too.

Parishioners are more than willing to give of their time *if* they have the time to plan for it and *if* they don't feel they are the last choice, the bottom of the barrel. Preregistration moves the recruitment of teaching personnel out of "asking for volunteers" and into the realm of God's call.

Jesus did not ask for volunteers to fill out the twelve; they were handpicked. Preregistration makes our handpicking easier.

Don't worry if you are unable to fill all the staff positions immediately. Even with publicity and promises, some people will hesitate. Registration Sundays in the fall will meet the remaining needs.

Third, preregistration allows us to ask more of people, not less. By painting the picture of God's educational ministry in the coming year, God is nicely served as he calls us to share our talents with one another, whether as teachers, staff assistants, or classroom helpers.

REGISTRATION IN THE FALL

Spring registration, though desirable, is *not* a necessity. Successful registration can be accomplished in the fall.

Fall registration works like this: Registration forms should be distributed to the general parish before the first registration Sunday. They can then be brought or sent to the parish office if, for some reason, the registrant family cannot attend on opening Sunday. The point is: *Get them.*

Set aside space for publicity in the Sunday bulletin and the weekly newsletter. Paint a broad picture of what is going to take place. Clergy can insert supporting illustrations into parish notices and printed sermons. Expect an atmosphere of anticipation to develop.

As the educational program is outlined, a chain of events begins. Parishioners commit their enthusiasms and hopes in concrete form by

Asking church members to participate as classroom teachers is made a lot easier if Sunday school is fun. To eyes of faith these photos catch a sign of God's ministry in our midst. Balloons can be one means of grace, and along with other ways to celebrate, detailed throughout this book, they all combine to make Sunday morning Christian education fun.

—offering themselves as teaching personnel, or

—offering their talents as resources.

In this way they stake a claim for themselves in the parish community of faith. Their personal commitment has solidly positive, concrete implications for parish stewardship. You can probably expect the Every Member Canvass to be more fruitful. It just makes sense. Where your heart and commitment are, there your treasure is also.

BUILDING A TEACHING TEAM

I like having a team of four to six teachers in each class. Under those circumstances the team members can work out their own schedules, and each carries his or her fair share of the load and responsibility.

The teaching schedules are not written in stone; because they emerge from team conversation, they are always amendable. They may also change as new teachers join in the fall. It is most important that each team be internally coherent—know itself as a unit and function as one—for it provides a providential statement of care, not only to the children in the class but to the children's parents.

Some team members may choose a term or two in which they will be primarily responsible for the teaching, some may work as assistants, and others may participate from time to time as they wait to move into a more active role later in the year.

A note of caution: There must be overlapping. Children need to know all their teachers, and vice versa. It is certainly unfair to "change horses in midstream," ending up with all new teachers and the children wondering what happened. If, however, an assistant of one term moves into the primary teaching position the next, and the other teacher gradually slips into another role or moves out for a term, the transition has been smoothly made.

The teachers can work out these teaching schedules among themselves. A few procedures for doing so are detailed in the All-Saints chapter, and an example of one team's teaching schedule follows.

TEACHER RECRUITMENT

The word "recruitment" is not the ideal one with which to describe the assembly of a Sunday-school teaching staff. It is God who

YEAR'S TEACHING SCHEDULE, GRADES 4 & 5
TEAM: Carolyn, Anne, Kathy, Bonnie

TERM'S THEME	MAJOR TEACHERS	RESOURCES
All Saints: Jacob	Carolyn, Anne (Kathy & Bonnie out)	Parents assist with drama, others with banner making
Christmas: Light coming into the world as seen in worship and our use of bread, study of symbols	Carolyn, Anne, Kathy (Bonnie out)	Parishioner breadmaker helped; parents help with Chrismons
Epiphany: Drama: Ahmal and the Night Visitors, Second half, Jesus' boyhood	Parents help with drama. Kathy, Bonnie, Carolyn led study of boyhood (Anne out)	Organist, a carpenter visits, trip to synagogue, slides on Palestine.
Lent: Jesus' ministry. Death. New life. Seeds and Easter egg tree.	Bonnie, Anne, Kathy (Carolyn out)	Puppet show on death. Parent help with Easter eggs.
Easter/Pentecost: Parables of Jesus	Carolyn, Kathy (Anne & Bonnie out)	Flower planting, stick puppets, dioramas

calls us to parish ministry—all of us, laity and clergy alike—and it is God who asks us to be involved in his educational ministry. God really is interested in helping us take care of ourselves.

Having determined the ages and number of students, handpick the four to six teachers needed to each class. The preregistration forms will help you find them.

A commitment to teach for only one of the terms is all right. If someone wants to teach all year, or for two or more terms, so much the better, but don't be pushy.

Some may prefer to offer background assistance and, instead of taking an active part in classroom leadership, provide supporting services. Artists may volunteer to help make Chrismons, and cooks may assist with breadmaking. All kinds of talents are revealed in the registration process. These assets are best collated and immediately published so that the entire parish family can begin to perceive the wealth of its interests. Enthusiasm is thereby given form and focus, and the year is off to a happy start. God is, I suspect, also pleased.

You may also find a number of teenagers volunteering to participate as teaching assistants. Encourage them. Except in rare cases they are not ready to assume the *primary* responsibility for class leadership, but they make able assistants, perhaps learning more than they were ever taught before. (Good teachers have always learned more than those they teach.)

Many teenagers are in a process psychologists call "negative identification." Because they are beginning to separate from their families, becoming their "own persons," whatever has to do with home, family, and church is, from time to time, in some disrepute to them. This attitude is indicative of a natural process of separation and individuation.

Teaching offers teens a way to move out of the "childhood" classroom and into the adult world of giving leadership. Others of their peers may register to take part in the adult class, or register for classes provided especially for their age group.

AN ENTHUSIASTIC START

The beginning of any program is a crucial time, because if the attitude of expectancy is lost it is almost impossible to regain; at best it is an uphill struggle. But if expectancy is encouraged and procedures are developed to help parents and other adults contribute their talents, spirited enthusiasm will likely continue. Festival worship supports it, and the fact that a congruence is felt between worship, study, and their common themes diminishes the tendencies toward isolation.

To initiate the fall program, offer a late-summer training session for everyone. Giving a dinner for the teaching personnel and their spouses is a warm gesture. Or serve simple refreshments, perhaps just coffee and dessert. Almost everyone loves a party. (If a person does not, it may be a reasonable indication that he or she may have trouble teaching.) Use name tags, and put copies of the year's program in everyone's hands.

Allow time for questions. Make particular note of the resources in the parish library and of the books suggested for each term. (The materials themselves can be examined later.)

Most importantly, this first meeting begins to forge staff life and excitement.

OPENING DAY AND TEACHER INSTALLATION

The opening day of fall's church school is going to be hectic; that is to be expected. Enjoy it; you could have an empty house.

In the chaos there is much excitement, the anticipation of being made new again.

Set up a big registration table in the parish hall. For those not previously registered, have parents and children fill out their forms and then have the kids go straight to meet their teachers. This is a Sunday for introductions, a time to say hello.

Ornament every member of the vestry or the governing board with a carnation. Note them in the bulletin, and make sure they are available to the parish family, giving directions, assisting at the registration tables, looking important and interested, and hearing the beat of parish life.

Name tags are essential as the newcomers are welcomed and the old-timers struggle to remember the names just on the tips of their tongues.

The second or third Sunday of the church-school year is a grand time to finish the registration and install the teaching staff.[1]

As a result of the registration, a large portion of the congregation will probably convene at the pulpit or altar-rail. Their numbers will be vivid witness to the parish family's wide-ranging interest in the Sunday school. Everyone is always pleasantly surprised and impressed, so plan the day carefully. Thoughtful preparations, expressions of enthusiasm, and everyone coming together after a summer's happy vacation are easily welded into joyful worship.

One parish newsletter sounded this celebratory note:

Opening Day

The only word to describe it is wonderful. The singing, combined choirs, E.T., endless lines to communion stations, flowers, balloons, banners, smiles, etc., etc., set the tone of one of our most festive occasions this year. We had a record breaking attendance, and our already crowded Christian Education facility was popping at the seams. Thanks to the many willing hands, our church school year is off to a splendid start.

A new day—a new beginning. Sounds refreshing.[2]

Not much question about what kind of year they were going to have, is there?

TRAINING THE TEACHING TEAM

After the teaching teams are convened, it is important to provide lots of support, and the best kind of support is good training. Clergy participation is crucial at this point.

Each complete team needs to meet for an evening session or two before the beginning of every term, or maybe once every calendar month throughout the year. In some parishes all the teaching teams meet with their clergy on weekday evenings, September through May.

By "complete team" I mean *every* person who will be involved in the year's teaching. These planning sessions, running a little over two hours, provide good adult Bible study, shared approaches to teaching, and confidence in the classroom. Always keep the simple Chinese adage in mind:

I hear and I forget.

I see and I remember.

I do and I understand.

What happens as a result of these meetings? The team members develop a spirit of camaraderie, and continuity is encouraged.

Occasionally a team member not actively teaching in the current term may find she or he can help with a special task for just one Sunday. That is mutual support at its best.

The children benefit, too, not only from the expertise these teachers bring but from the knowledge that the teaching team responsible for their class really is *their* team.

Also, a member of the clergy or lay staff of the parish ought to be assigned to each team as resource support. By lay staff I don't necessarily mean paid staff, for in every parish there are more than a few lay persons able to lead the discussions of the Bible.

No matter how one sees it, support for teaching teams lies at the heart of parish Christian education.

DEVELOPING A RESOURCE LIBRARY

Some churches do not have a Christian-education resource library, in others it is relegated to a back-hall closet. But on Sunday morning in many parishes it is the busiest place around. There are a hot pot

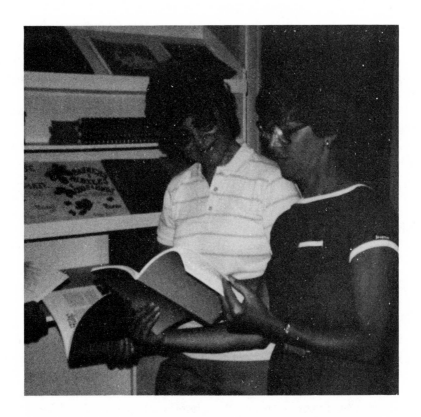

Teachers use the Christian education library at St. Andrew's Church in Meriden, Connecticut. The bright display of books not only commends browsing by teachers, but also encourages usage by children and parents. The shelves are angled at 45 degrees and have a ledge to stop. They alternate with horizontal shelves for stocking additional copies of the book displayed. Because of its bright colors and attractive pictures, the Arch Books Bible stories series, for example, lends itself to such an arrangement. If books encouraging Christian education are relegated to a back-room shelf or displayed haphazardly, parish Christian education is impoverished.

Sunday after-class teacher's meetings can convene around the library's array of books. As stories are briefly told about what worked in class and which books helped, resources and enthusiasm are generated for next week's journey in faith.

Just like the Christian education bulletin board and post-class staff meetings—when teacher questions can be answered and observations and joy shared—so too this library presentation of books strikes a clear reminder that God cares, Providence reigns, and Grace is near.

of coffee, maybe some doughnuts for the teachers, and much animated conversation about what has already happened or what is soon to happen. Enthusiasm is rapidly generated.

A library like this can be the centerpiece on the table of Christian education.

Be sure to set out in advance the books to be used in each term, and make them available to the teaching teams. Arrange them attractively for easy reference. If the books are simply filed on a shelf in the traditional manner, they probably will not get the attention they merit. The following illustration shows an alternative—a display case, which by its very openness invites curiosity.

A working library is essential to good parish Christian education.

TEACHER FUN AND FELLOWSHIP

This cadre of teaching teams and all its supporting members become, at best, a parish within the parish. There are Bible study, common tasks and ministry, shared vision, and the fellowship generated by affection and jobs well done.

When organized with care and with the clergy's active support, this group becomes a community others want to join. Word soon gets out that these teachers not only enjoy what they do but are learning even more about the Christian gospel than the children they teach.

In one parish the community of church-school teachers and their spouses meets quarterly for a potluck supper. A guest speaker discusses a biblical theme of current interest and its use in the classroom. These meetings provide practical help, along with a dose of good fellowship.

God's providence is the most appropriate phrase I know to describe his ministry at these meetings. I have been to some of them, and I have found that heightened trust, confidence, and joy are just a few of the teachers' responses to God's care.

This kind of organization takes parish energy and support—in short, commitment; there is no way around it. I hope you see it as a splendid opportunity to develop a vital parish life, and not just for the children but for everyone.

Notes

1. *The Book of Common Prayer* offers help at times of teacher

recognition and installation. The Commitment to Christian Service, page 421, and the Celebration of a New Ministry, page 559, provide formats within which teachers and students can be recognized. *The Book of Common Prayer, 1979.*

2. From the weekly newsletter *The Cathedral LOGOS* of St. Andrew's Cathedral, P. O. Box 1366, Jackson, MS 39205.

PART II

Taking Action:
Making the Vision Work

CHAPTER EIGHT

An Overview of the Year's Journey: Seasons and Festivals

When a parish knows where it is going and its vision is clear, trust, confidence, and excitement characterize its life.

This chapter maps the year's educational journey, from September to June, and reminds us of God's providential care for an educational enterprise belonging fundamentally to him.

THE ALL-SAINTS TERM

EARLY SEPTEMBER:

Parish registration.

MID-SEPTEMBER:

The *Celebration of the Ministry of Teaching*: the installation of the teaching staff.

Explorations center on what it means to be fully human. Study best concentrates on the lives of dedicated women and men from the past and present. We also begin to discern the shape of God's ministry in our midst, helping his world take care of itself. All saints, all of us.

OCTOBER:

All the saints pledge time, talents, and money to God's church work. Also, we are reminded that all our life is ministry to God, everywhere we work and play.

EARLY NOVEMBER:

The *All-Saints Festival*. Every class is encouraged to make a banner or other visual representation of their study. A parish reception in lieu of church-school class follows. The saints of God rejoice in their life together, as well as in God's presence.

THE CHRISTMAS TERM

MID-NOVEMBER:

The birth of Jesus approaches. Sights are turned to the promise of light and greatness to come.

LATER NOVEMBER:

Thanksgiving Day.

LATE NOVEMBER:

Foodstuffs, to be distributed by a local food agency, are presented at the offertory on the Sunday immediately after Thanksgiving Day.

Since many family members are home from school this weekend, worship becomes an especially powerful celebration. It is like a homecoming. The legacy of sharing at the time of Thanksgiving goes back far beyond the early settlers and the Indians, and it provides a moment of light to lives darkened by hunger.

EARLY DECEMBER:

The first Sunday in Advent. An Advent wreath appears. Light is coming for the world.

LATE DECEMBER:

The *Chrismon Festival*. Large Christmas trees are decorated with Chrismons (symbols of the Christ) made by the children in their classrooms.

Older children may choose to research the reasons these symbols are important in the life of the Church, and they may share their findings with the younger pupils. Intergenerational learning is rich activity.

A birthday party for Jesus follows in the parish hall.

THE EPIPHANY TERM

EARLY JANUARY:

>Light has entered the world, and the Church is formed.
>
>The term's focus is on communion, community, and the life of Jesus.

EARLY JANUARY:

>An opening *Epiphany celebration*. Epiphany celebrates the visit of the wise to Jesus. Just as the wise men brought gifts, so we bring them as well, presenting them at the creche. They will later be delivered to a local hospital's pediatrics unit, providing light for that world. An evening Feast of Lights is also good worship at its educational best.

LATE FEBRUARY:

>*"See and Believe" Sunday*. Having seen the light of God's Christ, some of the world believes. The story of the Transfiguration is our theme, and on this Sunday before Lent we may also celebrate with baptism, confirmation, and the Eucharist. The world responds to the light of the world by saying the "I will" of baptism. This might be a first communion for infant-baptized children.
>
>The celebration concludes with the *Shrove Tuesday* Pancake Supper.

THE LENTEN TERM

EARLY MARCH:

>*Ash Wednesday.*

EARLY MARCH:

>Studies concentrate on what it is to be "alive to God" in God's world. Jesus is our model, and his quality of life is the quality of life to which we are called. In Easter's shadow we explore the risking quality in Jesus' life, and we dare explore death, too.

MID-APRIL:

>The *Palm Sunday* Festival. Palm branches overhang a grand procession, and the Passion Gospel may end the Eucharist as the last gospel reading.

MID-APRIL:

> *Maundy Thursday.* In this evening service the altar and the church are stripped of color and ornament, and the candles are extinguished. Everything is darkened. Worship follows the Palm Sunday experience, fusing the ancient office of Tenebrae with the "Last Supper." This is powerfully visual worship.

MID-APRIL:

> *Easter Eve.* The celebration of God's light for the world.

MID-APRIL:

> The *Easter Sunday* Eucharist. The "dead" altar is dressed with color and candles, a cross may be flowered, and worship is the grandest of the year.

THE EASTER/PENTECOST TERM

MID-APRIL:

> The term's study centers on Jesus' resurrection appearances. Paul's life and ministry become useful vehicles as we take a close look at Jesus through his eyes.

LATE MAY:

> An *Ascension Day* theme. Jesus ascends, and we are left with special responsibilities for God's creation. Flowers and other green things may be planted in the *Rogation Sunday* tradition. A *Service for the Blessing of Animals* can be held on a Sunday afternoon.

EARLY JUNE:

> The *Pentecost Festival.* God's Spirit empowers Christians for life, and now we begin to return to the seasonal theme of the All-Saints term.
>
> *Graduation Day* for everyone. We take a three-month break because we need it, a "pause that refreshes."

CHAPTER NINE

The All-Saints Term:
All Saints, All of Us

Of all five terms, All-Saints is perhaps the most colorful. It may be by fire engines and rescue-squad trucks or by real-life saints telling their stories, but no matter how the color is generated, everything is brightened by a grand procession of saints in the early November festival.

WHY STUDY SAINTS?

All the world needs a hero. The celebration of sainthood falls within the realm of "hero worship."
Saints are models. One great hymn puts it this way,

> One was a doctor, one was a queen, one was a shepherdess on the green. . . ." There were soldiers and ". . . one was a priest, and one was slain by a fierce wild beast, and there's not any reason, no, not the least, why I shouldn't be one too.[1]

Each of us has a personality that is a composite of all the values, hopes, goals, and fears we hold. Learning from family life and from what his or her parents are like, a youngster's idea of a human being may turn out to be anything between two extremes. At one extreme is the idea of a giving, need-satisfying, anxiety-reducing, gentle person on whom the child can depend. At the other extreme is a rejecting peson, a dissatisfier who frequently elicits an anxiety, one who subjects the child to extended periods of frustration, someone on whom the youngster cannot depend. Even as I write this, I am aware of

these two extremess in my own parenting. Every child perceives his
or her parents this way. Children vary only in the way these percep-
tions are balanced.

Parents encourage personality formation by helping their children
choose playmates and by setting limits on their children's choices
when decisions are made that do not quite "measure up" to their
hopes and expectations.

For the most part personality is formed by interaction with significant persons around us, that is, those persons we feel are significant or have been designated as significant by a trusted authority, like
the Christian gospel or Church.

Role models are important, and the All-Saints term is a splendid
time to study persons the Church has, through the centuries, designated as exemplary of our humanity and God's love.

In a lovely way God becomes a playmate when children study the
lives of his saints, past and present, and through these explorations
the children are more fully formed as the human beings God created
them to be.

Year in and year out, by the time the children have been studying
for several years, they will have accrued not only a considerable
amount of information but a deep sensitivity to what it means to be
a Christian.

CHOOSING SOMEONE FROM THE PAST TO STUDY

The Bible is the best of all places to look for people to study, but
so too is the history of the Church, and a few suggestions from Church
history are listed in the Lenten-term section of this book.

Look also at recent American history, and the history of your local
community. At Grace Cathedral (Episcopal) in San Francisco, there
is a window dedicated to Albert Einstein, who opened new vistas for
all of us, a saint of God.

It is tough to say, but in this term refrain, if you can, from teaching
about Jesus. There are just too many other materials demanding our
attention, particularly the Old Testament stories. Besides, studies of
Jesus are the major foci of the next four terms.

If, however, you simply cannot resist exploring Jesus' good news,
see the Easter/Pentecost section and the Epiphany section (*Telling the
Good News Stories of Jesus*) of this book.

USING THE OLD TESTAMENT

Seven stories follow, six from the Old Testament and one from the New Testament. They suggest only a few of the many treasures in the Bible.

Once the stories to be taught are chosen, decisions have to be made about how many Sundays to spend with each. Better still, the entire church school can study the same person on a particular Sunday. That everyone is studying the same thing makes for simplicity. Here is where the seasonal approach to Sunday-school organization shines.

We learn best when teaching and learning are clearly focused on as few things as necessary.

> In one year's class, Jacob tricking Esau was the Bible story of choice for several Sundays. The team of teachers carefully developed the story, and this is one of the tools they used.
>
> Brownies were secretly made without sugar, and cold coffee substituted for coke. And after the first bite deceit became the burning issue for the class. Children were led to talk out their feelings in relation to Esau and his brother, and finally they ate and drank the real things.
>
> But still later one of these fourth graders took a "bad" brownie home and gave it to his dad, enjoyably reading the Sunday sports section.
>
> It was a lovingly hostile gesture designed to get attention. And it did. You can imagine what happened next, with the first crunch and sudden shock.
>
> But as I heard it later, part of what transpired was an enthusiastic explanation of the morning's learning. And both mom and dad liked that.

Clearly this teaching team was making good use of the adage introduced in chapter 5:

I hear and I forget.

I see and I remember.

I do and I understand.

Concordia's *Arch Books* series includes the following titles. Each of these brief booklets contains bright pictures and can be easily read.

A "Note to Parents" at the end of each not only helps classroom teaching but can assist with home study.[2]

1. *The Great Promise* Genesis 12:1–21:3). Abraham's story of great faith and God's promise to him.

2. *The Wicked Trick* and *The Farmer Takes a Wife* (Genesis 27–29:28. The story of how Jacob tricked his brother and of how he, in turn, was deceived by his father-in-law.

3. *The Boy Who Saved His Family* (Genesis 34–50). The story of Joseph and his brothers, and the themes of jealousy, love, and forgiveness.

4. *The Great Escape* (Exodus 3:1–15:1). God works with Moses to set his people free.

5. *The Boy with a Sling* (1 Samuel 16:1–18:5). The story of David and Goliath.

6. *A Story for Obed* (Book of Ruth). The story of Naomi and Ruth, two of Jesus' forebears, and of how kindness was rewarded.

7. *The Man Who Changed His Name* (Acts 9:1–30). The story of St. Paul continues Easter/Pentecost's study.

No matter which biblical figure you choose, the most important thing is not the factual situation (what he or she did and how) but the central theme of love and God's care, and the sense of duty and compassion each manifested in his or her life.

Maybe you would prefer to study St. Paul. If so, there is an abundance of materials suggested by the Easter/Pentecost and Epiphany terms, all of them ready to use. As important as St. Paul is, however, there are many others, and they constitute a formidable list:[3]

 —St. Andrew
 —St. Thomas
 —St. Stephen, Deacon and Martyr (see also the Lenten term)
 —St. John
 —The Holy Innocents (see also the Epiphany term)
 —The Confession of St. Peter
 —The Conversion of St. Paul (see also the Epiphany and Easter/
  Pentecost terms)
 —St. Matthias
 —St. Joseph (see also the Epiphany term)
 —St. Mark
 —St. Philip and St. James
 —St. Barnabas
 —Nativity of St. John the Baptist (see also the Christmas term)
 —St. Mary the Virgin (see also the Christmas term)

—St. Bartholomew
—St. Matthew
—St. Michael
—St. Michael and All the Angels
—St. Luke
—St. James of Jerusalem, Brother of Jesus and Martyr
—St. Simon and Saint Jude
—All-Saints Day

CHOOSING SOMEONE FROM TODAY TO STUDY

The All-Saints term also lends itself to an exploration of our occupations. We are, all of us, saints of God, and God uses our jobs to help us take care of one another and his world.

For adolescents, this term is an opportunity to explore how they might spend their lives as adults. For adults, it can happily center on God's providential care (through us) of his world and on the ways in which he has called us to our occupations.

Schedule Police Canine Corps, Fire Department, or Rescue Squad members for Sunday visits. And expand this list, for teaching like this is bright.[4]

What happens when this kind of teaching takes place? God sparks the hearts and minds of our children with interest.

> One year a fireman remarked on the occasion of his Sunday visit,
> "I never thought of myself as a saint."
> A year later he was baptized.

God moves in his world in quiet, caring ways, bringing his people to new life.

Members of other professions can also be scheduled to address Sunday-school classes. It all depends on what is revealed in the registration forms. An electrician, for example, might hook up a simple circuit and describe how she helps God take care of the world. Or an artist might sketch some impressions of the class and talk about the ministry of creating beauty in God's world. Use your imagination, but make use of the parish, for God's sake; it is a treasure of a resource.

> One year John Stewart, veterinarian extraordinaire, visited classes with his dog Sam. He showed his skill, talked about the care of animals, and explained in his own words how he believed he was serving God in his daily job.

Firemen Spark Interest In Learning About Saints

VIRGINIA BEACH — When the fire engines came to Eastern Shore Chapel, they came not to put out a fire but to light one.

Their attendance at church was part of the Chapel's Christian education program which ignited a spark in the minds of many three, four and five-year-old Sunday schoolers who were trying to understand the concept of sainthood.

While their older classmates studied historically significant saints, the younger children learned about "modern-day saints" in preparation for the celebration of All Saints Day in the church recently.

In addition to the visit from the fire department, the three, four and five-year-olds have had visits from the Rescue Squad, the Police Department and Canine Corps and a doctor. The children were encouraged to follow the example of these community workers and to be "helpers" too.

"Saints of a long time ago are hard for little children to relate to," explained Mrs. Carrollyn Cox, Christian Education Consultant at the Chapel.

"We felt young children could better understand the concept of sainthood with present-day people who exhibit the same traits of loyalty and preserverance the saints did."

The older children made banners about the saints to carry into church in the All Saints procession Sunday. The younger ones marched in the procession dressed in simple costumes depicting modern-day saints.

Small doctors, firepersons, policepersons, nurses, rescue squad spersons and other assorted community helpers filled into church in what at times resembled a Halloween parade rather than what is generally thought of as a church service.

As part of the service, the children gathered in their costumes

Becoming a Fireman Might Help Scott Wall Become a Saint

in the chancel to sing a children's hymn, "I Sing a Song of the Saints of God."

Dressing in costume was also felt to be an appropriate way for the children to begin to learn the relationship between Halloween and the church calendar, Mrs. Cox said.

Though it was celebrated by the children on Sunday All Saints Day itself is on Nov. 1. October 21, Halloween, used to be called All Hallows Eve (hallow, meaning holy ones).

"There was one little boy who was determined to come dressed in his Halloween costume and of all things it was a devil," said Mrs. Cox, laughing. "But even if this little boy didn't get the relationship quite straight, he certainly has benefited from seeing people who help people in action."

Other Students See Careers as Policemen and Construction Workers

He later thanked the teacher for asking for his help. "It was one of the nicest things I ever did. Nobody's ever used me as a saint before."

Dr. Stewart was also able to describe some of the decisions he made along the way that got him to vet school, and speculated about the way he believed God nudged his interest here and there—which included the support of his wife.

I wonder about the number of children who, in those Sunday morning moments, were stirred by God to begin to consider taking care of animals in the work-for-pay future. We may never know, but God does. And rejoices.

Or a member of the medical helping professions might give a simple physical with a stethoscope; St. Luke's feast day falls on the eighteenth of every October, and tradition has it that Luke was a physician. The Sundays closest to his day are good ones to explore the way God is with us through the lives of those he has called to healing ministries—nurses, physicians, social workers, counselors, and so on.

Your visiting saints may be better able to talk about how they help God take care of his world than about how God worked with them as they choose their jobs. Perhaps you can suggest how God's call developed, using a bit of Bible-imaginative speculation. Simply look for the signs of early interest, how and when doors opened, and why decisions were made for one thing and against another.

Most Christians are able, given these few guidelines and a helpful conversation with another, to speculate about God's presence and ministry in the decisions they made about their jobs. This discussion will probably necessitate a meeting before class.

Ideally, those who assist in this kind of teaching will dress as they do at work.

I hope you will also consider encouraging the participation of men or women in occupations usually associated with the other sex only. (At one time we had to search hard to find women in the legal profession.) Many of our attitudes about life develop because of the things we study, and by portraying men as the only persons who use their heads or hands in work-for-pay, we give pupils a lopsided picture of life. That is unacceptable in the teaching of maturing children.

Children begin at an early age to pose questions about their life's work, and this term's study assists God as he brings the questions up.

I hope you will also use parents as teachers. They are saints too, and the most important persons in the children's lives.

THE BOTTOM LINE IS: God uses educational events to "spark"

our interest in our futures, and with only a little bit of Bible-imagi-native speculation we can begin to conceive just a bit more fully who participated with us in the decisions we made about the work we do.

GOD'S MINISTRY AND OUR CHOICE OF OCCUPATIONS

Robert Frost put it this way:

Two roads diverged in a wood, and I—
I took the one less traveled by,
And that has made all the difference.

Why do we take one road and not another? Why do we choose one job over another? Is it only chance, or simple good fortune, or good luck?

Give an infinite number of monkeys an infinite number of typewri-ters and one of them will come up with *King Lear.*

Or is it providence?

I believe providence plays a part, and so do many other Christians. God is with us every day, and he *is* interested in our lives and the ways we earn our daily bread. For better and for worse God weds himself to us.

God is even more interested in the way we earn our daily bread than we are. Our primary concerns are ourselves and those closest to us, but God is equally concerned with all of us. God wants the life of the world to sound more like a symphony than a cacophony. Yet with each of us looking out for number one, the latter is more likely; just look at the morning newspaper.

But still the symphony sounds—to the faithful a sure sign of God's presence and ministry among us, always and everywhere. God is with us, as close as breath is to the lungs.

Conversation, from the Latin *con* (with) and *versari* (to travel), describes this ministry. A great old hymn puts it this way: "He walks with me, and he talks with me. . . ." God is not silent; he never has been and never will be. "Conversationalist" is one of the best terms by which to describe him. Clearly he is a conversationalist throughout Scripture, and another way to conceive of Jesus is as God's conver-sational ministry in the flesh. In other words, if you want to know what God's ubiquitous conversation with us sounds like, just read what Jesus said.

God is one in dialogue with us always and everywhere, stirring our hearts and enlightening our minds.[5]

ALL SAINTS, ALL OF US

Saints are not goody-goodies. They never have been and they never will be, and we diminish them and ourselves when we pass them off as such. Though the following cartoon is delightful, it is not a fair representation either of who we are or who God is.

A saint is a responsible person, someone just like you and me, who, with God, helps the world take care of itself. Someone just like John Stewart.

Why is it we choose the occupations we do? Is it simply luck or chance, or is it an expression of God's care for his world? I believe the latter, for helping with our choice is God's second most important ministry to us (his most important ministry being that of calling us into a knowledgeable relationship with him).

Occupation is our daily work, the way we spend our time in service to the world. All of us need to work—that is a given. Nevertheless we tend to look for jobs that "fit" us. Why? Just to feel better? That is certainly part of the equation, but not the only part. We look for jobs that seem to make a good as use as possible of the unique combination of talents each of us possesses. Hence, we carefully consider every possible employment.

I suspect our side of the occupational deliberation with God follows this order:

1. Our talents, hopes, and aspirations.
2. The work opportunities before us.
3. The *needs of God's world.*

We human beings tend to think first about what we need, even at the expense of the world around us. There is a natural concordance with the "survival of the fittest" imprinted in each of us.

God's deliberations with us are, however, framed differently. God values us as the beloved persons we are, but he is equally concerned with the welfare of his world. Hence, his deliberations start with ours but interchange the second and third factors thus:

1. Our talents, hopes, and aspirations.
2. The *needs of his world.*
3. The work opportunities before us.

God loves us *and* the world, and his deliberations with us reflect

"*When people ask what you're like, I say you're a saint. That usually shuts them up.*"

Drawing by Frascino; © 1978, The New Yorker Magazine, Inc. Distributed in *Laity Exchange*, No. 4. July 1978.

it. We are, of course, free to choose our jobs for ourselves, but God is a participant in all our deliberations.

One can look at the balance of occupations in any given society and see it in terms of supply and demand, or cultural imperatives, or even as the result of simple greed. We have so many plumbers because of a demand for their services, and so many nurses, or lawyers, or garbage collectors for the same reason. Simple greed or intellectual capability might be why these jobs are chosen, but there is more involved.

Given the human freedom to choose our own way, God attempts to wed the talents of his people and the opportunities for employment to the needs of his world. His is a ministry seeking to bring the people of his world, each unique, into symphonic communion.

"But," you ask, "what about those who aren't happy with what they're doing?" Granted, some of us are not, maybe because of talents left unused or because our present job was the only one we could get. Does this mean God is not involved? Heaven forbid. Given human freedom and the constraints God has placed on his power, sometimes the "best" is simply not possible.

Happily, though, even "not the best" or "the worst" can be seen as "good" when we carefully consider the five billion people in the world and God's complex job of conducting a symphony while each of us instrumentalists all too blithely plays our own tune.

God's spirit participates in the world's household in a pervasive and careful way, and our diverse occupations are signs of the effectiveness of his presence and ministry. God will not coerce the people of his world into taking particular jobs; that kind of force is not of him.[6] Rather, he participates in every decision, conversationally keeping company with each of us, celebrating our talents and hopes and attempting to open up employment possibilities that match the household's needs as well as our hopes and aspirations.

Every parish is a treasure house full of signs of God's ministry. So is every community surrounding the local church. Our balance of occupations is a sign of God's hand at work in his world, making things more a symphony than a cacophony.

I hope you will consider the way God conversed with you about your job(s) in his world, for THE BOTTOM LINE IS: This kind of preparation will enable you, when you schedule some of God's saints, to help your pupils see (by using Bible-imaginative speculation) God's ministry in occupational decisions.

It is Christian education at its best.

A SAMPLING OF CLASSROOM ACTIVITIES

1. *Adopting a Shut-in.* Along with saints past and present, I hope you will include those older parishioners in your parish whom most of us call "shut-ins." Your class may want to take one of these persons into your common life on Sunday morning, perhaps by "adoption." Though the "shut-ins" may never be physically present, you can remember them at special times of the year, perhaps by sharing with them some of the things you are doing in the classroom or by making pictures and banners for them.

Should you choose this ministry, your class will learn something about compassion and caring and perhaps, when these parishioners share their personal stories, gain some notion of reverence for a life well spent. In so doing, you will be a part of the great Church ministry of visitation and care. Maybe clergy can accompany you from time to time to celebrate a home communion.

2. *Chancel Drama.* For those teachers who want to accept it, Sunday's main worship offers an opportunity for chancel drama. I have seen, for instance, Queen Esther save her people and, on another Sunday, the walls of Jericho come tumbling down. Attendance always markedly increases for these events.

With only a little work the plays can be done well. Lines need not even be memorized; instead, one or two persons can read the story in dialogue. Costuming and placement are fun to arrange, and easy, too. And help is readily available: Just look at the registration forms.

With a little advance consultation the day's preacher can, after the performance, summarize the drama's chief points. Or he or she can place a short homily within the play's context, creating a powerful expression of God's Word.

For classes that have chosen this approach, almost all teaching and learning revolves around the play. By the time the rehearsals have begun, several people probably will have signed up to help with such things as costuming, direction, and production. Teenagers love this work.

3. *Creating a Bright Banner.* The planning and construction of a banner for term-ending festivals are good tasks around which to plan classroom activity.

A class of teenagers once put together a magnificent collage on the theme of love, basing it on the Book of Ruth and using magazine illustrations. At other times three-dimensional displays have been constructed.

A first-grade class may want to make individual banners the size of sheets of writing paper (they are much easier for the little people to handle).

A note of caution: Please let these creations be as much the children's work as possible. There is a fine line between encouraging the young artists to do their best (helping them to develop their talents fully) and taking over the creation of the banner. Sometimes the latter may be appropriate, but only in the closing seconds of the eleventh hour.

Use your imagination. And have fun.

DESIGNING CLASSROOM ACTIVITY: THINGS TO KEEP IN MIND

A seasonal approach to Christian education offers this bonus: Because All-Saints is the overriding theme during the first six weeks of the year, the sainthood theme ties all the Sundays together.

Because all the Sunday-school classes are working on the same seasonal theme, teachers may unexpectedly hear that another class has done something they would like to try. Try to be flexible enough to drop a planned activity in favor of a spontaneous one.

It is also important to develop the term's curriculum so that each Sunday can stand on its own as much as possible. Some children attend church-school sporadically, and irregular attendance can, unfortunately, disable those carefully planned lessons that build on the previous week's work. If one Sunday's class depends too much on another's, a lot of time will be spent "catching up" the children who were absent the week before. To many teachers this means they must deal with their (legitimate) anger as their conscientiously developed lesson plans slide "down the drain." Don't get caught in this bind.

The adult class can explore sainthood, too. The discussions can center on some of the biblical figures listed earlier in this book, or on the way God works with us in choosing the jobs we hold (or wish we held but don't), or on how certain qualities in the lives of saints illuminate the hard work of being parents.

THE ALL-SAINTS FESTIVAL

The term ends "with a bang." The joy of the day emerges from the life, vitality, enthusiasm, and spirited exploration that were evoked as we (all of us, together) studied the saints.

I urge classes to consider making a banner about a saint, past or present. Perhaps the most satisfying event in a Sunday service is a grand procession of teachers and children carrying banners.

One year an upper-grade class brought guitarists to accompany the three-, four-, and five-year-olds in the first verse of "I Sing a Song

of the Saints of God."[7] Then the whole congregation thundered in for
the last two verses, with trumpets hitting the high notes. The expan-
sion of voices and volume, the adult congregation singing with and
under the children's voices, was a powerfully dramatic moment. It
made the effect of the Peace, immediately following, especially keen.

Happy planning with an eye toward celebration enables this kind
of worship to take place. Because information on the festival was
published in the parish newsletter (along with other news about what
was going on in the Sunday-morning classroom), anticipation had
grown. As I said before, it is hard to stand on the curb when a parade
band comes marching by.

HUNDREDS OF IDEAS FOR JUST SIX WEEKS

The seasonal approach to Sunday-morning Christian education
generates hundreds of ideas for the classroom. If you have ever wondered what you are going to do next, just take a look at the possibilities
listed below, all of which make for creative Christian education.

FIRST SUNDAY:

—Register the children.
—Meet your class; share who you are, your family story, what
   you like to eat. Ask the pupils to reciprocate. No matter what
   the age group, introductions are crucial, an indispensable part
   of Christian formation.
—Choose a saint to study.
—Begin to discuss banners. And remember, they must be im-
   portant-looking (four to six feet long).
—Check out a book on making banners.
—Look over the list of parish talents (culled from the registration
   forms).
—Who would like to decorate the Christian-education bulletin
   board for the term?
—Schedule your teaching team's meetings.

SECOND SUNDAY:

—Registration continues, and introductions, too.
—Schedule parish saints.
—What community saints would you like to have?
—You should have picked your special saint(s) for study.

—Begin making a banner.

—Do you want to adopt a parish shut-in?

—Would you like to schedule a dramatic presentation in Sunday's worship?

—Who will host the All-Saints festival party?

—What about the Christian-education bulletin board?

—Learn the "Saints of God" hymn with the organist.

—Would you like the choir to help your children learn to sing?

—Shall you write a litany for the festival?

—How about planning a drama for the fifth Sunday's liturgy?

—Can parents help in your class?

—Check the Christian-education library.

THIRD SUNDAY:

—Policemen or firemen may visit; they can be scheduled by someone in the office.

—Consider baking bread for the Eucharist and presenting it at the Offertory.

—What about banners?

—Are you learning and discussing a hymn?

—Schedule a parish saint.

—Study your particular saint.

—Discover the qualities of being a saint.

—How are your children saints?

—Who will host the festival party?

—Small children might begin to think about dressing as saints (modern and old) for the festival.

—The Christian-education bulletin board should be up.

—Look over the talents listed on the registration forms. Can you use any of them?

—Begin to think about light and darkness in the Christmas term. How are saints "light to the world"?

FOURTH SUNDAY:

—The policemen or firemen visit.

—Parish saints can visit your class.

—Can you use your clergy for a presentation?

—Learn a hymn and discuss it.

—Can you use the choir and the organist?

—Who are some modern saints?

—How is your banner coming?

—Bake bread for the Eucharist and present it.
—Discover the qualities of the saints of God.
—Think about doing the Christian-education bulletin board for the pre-Advent series on light and darkness.
—How are saints "light to the world"?
—Have you done any drama?
—Would an older class be willing to do a play for a younger class (or the adult class)?
—Are you complimenting your children?

FIFTH SUNDAY:

—Continue to schedule parish saints.
—What will you present in the festival?
—How is the banner coming?
—Final plans should be made for the parish party.
—Introduce the theme of light and darkness, to be assumed after All Saints.
—How do saints "light" the world today?
—Who are some modern saints?
—Who are the persons who "darken" our world?
—Have you used the organist?
—Have you made use of the clergy?
—Do you need some parents to help with the banners?
—Have you used the specially talented people to help with the banners?
—Have you adopted a shut-in?

SIXTH SUNDAY:

—The rescue squad can visit.
—Continue to study your chosen saint, or move on to another.
—How are class order and discipline? Do you need to consult with others about them?
—How about light and darkness?
—Parish saints?
—A banner or costumes—which will it be?
—Who will bake bread and present it on the day of the festival?
—Have fun with your class.
—Have you used the Christian-education library?
—Wonder with your children about how *they* are saints in their world.
—How are their parents saints?

—Will you share some of your learning with the shut-in you adopted?

—Describe the impending festival.

—Do you need help with the banner?

—Invite parents to look at your banner next Sunday after class.

SEVENTH SUNDAY:

—Finish the banner and plan for the party.

—Take your class to church so they can see where they shall be sitting.

—Take your class to church so they can see how the great procession will move.

—Ask the church-school coordinator to explain things.

—Have a parish saint visit.

—Who is going to bake bread and present it next week?

EIGHTH SUNDAY:

—The All-Saints Festival and parish party.

Notes

1. *The Hymnal of the Protestant Episcopal Church, 1940* (New York: The Church Pension Fund, 1940), Hymn 243.

2. Arch Books (St. Louis, MO: Concordia Publishing House, 1971).

3. *The Bible, The Book of Common Prayer,* and *Lesser Feasts and Fasts* (a calendar—with collects, psalms, and lessons—published by Seabury Press), all of which contain ample materials for study. A sampling of saints can be found in the Episcopal Church calendar, on page 921 of *The Book of Common Prayer.*

4. "Firemen Spark Interest in Learning about Saints," *The Virginia Beach Beacon,* 8 November 1976. Published as part of *The Ledger-Star* and *The Virginian-Pilot,* Norfolk, VA.

5. *The Book of Common Prayer, 1979.* "On Grace," 858.

6. *The Hymnal of the Protestant Episcopal Church, 1940,* Hymn 298.

7. Ibid., Hymn 243.

CHAPTER TEN

The Christmas Term:
Out of the Darkness . . .
Light

Christmas naturally evokes the most enthusiasm of all five terms. At least two factors contribute to this feeling: First, with its bright procession of banners and lively music, the All-Saints festival builds interest and excitement. Second, Thanksgiving is only a stone's throw away, and Christmas Day just beyond it. No matter how young or old we are, memories are being called to life.

PREPARING FOR CHRISTMAS

The Christmas term poses special organizational problems, chiefly because there is a wealth of materials available, far more than we can deal with in only seven weeks.

The four-week Advent season has always centered on two themes: (1) light coming into a dark world, and (2) the events surrounding Jesus' birth. But this is simply too much material to handle in the short period of four weeks. So do this: move the explorations of light and darkness into the Sundays of November, leaving the month of December for a more leisurely exploration of the Advent, or coming of Jesus, and call November pre-Advent. This artificial distinction makes learning less harried and much more enjoyable than it would otherwise be.

TWO MIDTERM FESTIVALS

Parish festivals always generate enthusiasm, and two special possibilities occur as the season of Pentecost draws to a close. Both illustrate the themes of darkness and light.

1. *Christ the King.* The Sunday of Christ the King falls on the first Sunday immediately after Thursday's Thanksgiving Day. So, you ask, how does this help us?

Pentecost began in the early summer with a great deal of happy enthusiasm. Jesus' healing ministry appeared regularly. But this joyful note is (subtly at first, later more fully) amended to include a note of God's judgment.

If everything were all right with the world there would be no need for a saving person to come among us. Hence, Pentecost's theme is cast differently in October and November than it was in June and July. This different "cast" warns us that all is not right in God's world.

The whole of the Church year moves toward the Sunday of Christ the King. From Advent and Christmas we are moved toward Calvary's death, Easter's life, and the day of Pentecost. God's Christ presides over all things, and, though we live yet in a disordered world, his is a ruling ministry that orders our world. Jesus is Christ the King.

2. *Thanksgiving Day.* Thanksgiving Day also follows at November's end.

On the Sunday after Thanksgiving—which is also the Sunday of the victorious Christ, members of the parish might, along with the church school community, present canned and/or dry goods for distribution through your community's Emergency Food Pantry.

Details need to be carefully planned for whole family participation, but communion time provides a particularly dramatic moment for the presentation. Food can be brought to the altar rail and offered at the Lord's table. As the collection grows the reminder is vivid: as God feeds us so, too, He feeds the world, often through us. His table is a large one, infinitely more expansive than any altar.

There's also a note of judgment in this Thanksgiving action. For part of what's brought home is a deeper understanding that many persons in God's world have suffered the loss of the basic human right to eat nutritiously, or even to eat at all.

ORGANIZING LESSONS FOR THE CHRISTMAS TERM: A GUIDE

There are a ton of store-bought religious education materials available for this term, but maybe you'd like to develop your own. They would certainly cost less, and it's easy.

Two lists of lessons designated Tract I and Tract II follow. They are guidelines for organizing the Christmas term. Remember, though, there are only seven weeks for classes; so plan carefully.

LESSONS	TRACT I	TRACT II
First Sunday	John 1:1–5	Isaiah 42:5–9
Second Sunday	Isaiah 42:5–9	Isaiah 45:4–7
Third Sunday	Isaiah 9:2–7 or Matthew 4:15–16	Isaiah 60:1–5, 7d
Thanksgiving Day		
Fourth Sunday	Luke 1:26–38	Luke 1:26–38
Fifth Sunday	Luke 1:39–49	Luke 1:39–49
Sixth Sunday	Luke 2:1–20	Luke 1:13–17, 36–37, 57–80
Chrismon Sunday	Matthew 1:18–25	Luke 2:1–20

Tract II is elaborated in the following section, just to demonstrate how easy it is to organize biblical verses and stories for study, but even in the best of times you will never be able to cover all the materials in just seven weeks.

DON'T TRY TO "TEACH IT ALL"

Almost all of us struggle with wanting to be ultraresponsible. Do not expect to "teach it all"—whatever "it all" is—this year (or any year, for that matter). Simply enjoy the exercise of planning consecutive Sundays' study. And remember, less is often more.

Next year's teachers will probably cover similar material in a different way, and both approaches will have a positive impact on the Christian education of your pupils. Work at a comfortable pace, take it easy, and enjoy yourself and your students.

NOVEMBER'S PRE-ADVENT: OUT OF THE DARKNESS . . .

In the weeks before Christmas every worship lectionary makes use of the Old Testament prophets. They often described God's immediacy in terms of light.

Israelite prophets, like Isaiah, arose from the friction between two cultures. One culture worshiped the Lord of History, and the others worshiped gods of the earth, the *baals.*

The God of Israel was no Canaanite *baal.* As Lord of History God made himself known in a series of unique events, beginning with Moses and the Hebrew people's exodus from Egypt. He established a covenant with a particular people, and to them he gave the mission of making him known in the world. Hence, the Israelite prophets began their oracles, "Thus says the Lord." Through the prophets God called on Israel to hear, and light to a dark world was one of the images of which they heard.

First Sunday: Isaiah 42:5–9. These verses recall the story of creation (from Genesis 1) and God's promise that he would bring light into his world again, though the next time perfectly. You might want to spend some time on the biblical accounts of creation and of the making of light, dry land, etc.

Second Sunday: Isaiah 45:4–7. Because of his new light, God says: You will know

> there is no other, beside me there is no God. I form light and create
> darkness, I am the Lord, who does all things.

This is another reference to the story of creation.

Third Sunday: Isaiah 60:1–5, 7d. This lesson opens with the words, "Arise, shine; for your light has come, and the glory of the Lord has risen upon you."

The next Sunday begins the lighting of the Advent wreath.

Thanksgiving Day: Nehemiah 8:10.

POSSIBILITIES FOR PRE-ADVENT TEACHING

Light and darkness are the themes for the three weeks after All Saints.

How can we construct studies to move us into this great biblical theme?

Enthusiasm for the saints may still be evident. If so, capitalize on it. Continue to explore how past saints were light for the dark world, and how their lives are light to us yet. This focus may require some research of those who did not teach during the All-Saints term, but the materials are readily available.

All of us want to "see" clearly; it is a desire basic to human life. But there is much more to the exploration of light than just seeing or not seeing.

A small part of every one of us fears the dark. The older we get, the more easily this fear can be ignored. But still, just as a small child waking at night and crying out for a reassuring parent fears the dark, much of the Christian journey centers around our yearning for "a lamp unto our feet" (Psalm 119:105f).

Once during this November period several parish artists, discovered in the registration process, made sketches on the theme of light and darkness. Later they used paint, colored glass, candles, and paper cut-outs. They had fun applying the talents they loved, and the teenagers with whom they worked were impressed, not only with the drawing but with what they learned from these dedicated artists about judgment and sinfulness.

Young children may paint a small area of paper with yellow watercolor, then cover the whole sheet with black crayon. After trading papers, all try to uncover the "light" by scratching off the "dark," discussing both their activity and their feelings as they "see the light."

POINT: Public-school teachers can be of great help by contributing ideas similar to those described above. Ask them.

A puppeteer, again discovered through the parish registration, once worked out puppet plays on light and darkness. They were scheduled on several Sundays.

I was surprised, walking by a third-grade classroom one Sunday, to see forty children and teachers sitting in absolute silence. The room didn't usually lend itself to such stillness.

I later discovered the crowd was occasioned by the addition of the fourth and fifth grades. The play itself, lasting only five or six minutes, was good preparation for later discoveries in the classroom.

The teachers of the two older grades had decided, after hearing of the play in the teacher's staff meeting the previous Sunday, to join the younger grade. Preparations were made by telephone during the week, and follow-up exercises had already been developed to bring home some of the learnings.

As I recall, the play vividly demonstrated the way in which dark-

ness can engulf everything and, through friendly puppets, the manner in which even a tiny light can illuminate.

And every one of these teachers was making good use of the adage:

> I hear and I forget.
>
> I see and I remember.
>
> I do and I understand.

New strategies are always taking shape as we teach, and when everyone is working around the same seasonal theme we can readily share them.

Two heads are better than one, says the old saw, and a seasonal approach to Christian education multiplies those heads by the number of teachers and parents involved.

A SECOND-GRADE LESSON PLAN FOR
"OUT OF THE DARKNESS . . ."

POINT: Teaching biblical themes is more difficult than merely telling a Bible story. Thematic teaching is difficult for three reasons: (1) Generally there is no story line to guide the pupils, (2) there may be no clear way to personalize the lesson, and (3) abstract teaching in the Sunday-school classroom almost always fails. There is, however, a simple solution to this problem.

The following lesson plan illustrates how a second-grade teacher took the theme of light and darkness and (1) developed a story line around it and (2) personalized it. The story line was about the part light plays in everyday life. The pupils' own experiences made it personal.

With just a little imaginative speculation, thematic teaching is easy. And here is where teaching teams work best, because two heads are generally better than one.

This second-grade teacher—like many others at work in the Sunday-morning classroom—is not a professional teacher, but her love for pupils, and just a little imaginative care, led her to formulate the following plan:

SUBJECT:
Study of light imagery: pre-Advent.

PURPOSE:

To acquaint my students with scripture passages which appear during this part of the liturgical year, and to draw parallels between their references to light and light as it appears in our everyday living.

METHOD:

Appointed Bible passages were read to the class, along with the Collect for the Day from the Book of Common Prayer. (Prayer Books are available, and every week we spend some time exploring a few of its pages. Right after the reading of the day's lesson and collect, the Lord's Prayer is also used.)

Students were asked to stop the teacher in her reading when she reached a word that meant something equivalent or similar to the word "light." I also explained that the words they were about to hear were not necessarily ones with which they might be readily familiar . . . that is, they would not be words like "sunshine," "lightning," etc.

A teenage assistant wrote all the words they collected on the blackboard as we went along through the reading. And by the end of the reading a formidable list of words had been placed on the board. I reiterated that all of those words meant light.

I then asked my students to choose one of the words, and to draw a picture of it. I emphasized that there were many other words (other than those listed on the board) which could also be illustrated as light. One student asked that "love" be added to the list. It was placed on the board.

Students were then asked how they felt when they were experiencing and living these words. Their feelings were now reflected in the drawings on which they were now working. To emphasize that all of the words did indeed mean light, each student wrote the word "light" in the upper left-hand corner of their paper. Those that worked faster designed several drawings, although they were asked to select a different word each time.

The list of words we selected follows:

joy	praise	spirit
mighty	God (2)	prepare the way
Lord (8)*	forgive	light (2)
good news	breath	deliver
sing	salvation	righteousness
kingdom	open	grace
glory	love	

*The number of times these words were selected.

Some of the drawings showed children playing together, persons at worship, eating pizza and drinking coke, helping mommy at home, going to parties, and one was even a picture of me![1]

For other classes this may not be the most helpful tool; a more physical approach might better create situations in which minds can open themselves to learning.

One activity might be to blindfold some older students and then note their attempts to do simple tasks and to move around a room (in the dark, as it were).

Similarly, other classes might darken a room as much as possible, then light a central candle and pass its flame to candles held by everyone else. This multiplication of light is often picked up in an Epiphany Feast of Lights, celebrating the twelfth day of Christmas.

Older pupils might be interested in preparing a dramatic presentation for the younger set, or even for the adult class. A presentation for the latter gives the adults a chance to apprise themselves of what is happening in their children's education.

Note: Decisions about these possibilities must be made before the term begins.

DECEMBER'S ADVENT: GOD'S LIGHT FOR THE WORLD

There is much important material in these four weeks, so you must make some hard decisions about just what you intend to cover because you cannot cover it all, there is simply not enough time.

Much of the Christmas story is, naturally, taught in the preparations for the Christmas pageant. Each year the pageant can be rewritten to incorporate various parts of the whole story.

During Advent's Sundays some classes may want to study their families, taking a cue from the scriptural readings just noted. Siblings, grandparents, parents, friends in the neighborhood—all populate a world unique to each child. Photographs can be gathered from scrapbooks and displayed, or pictures can be drawn. In many cases it might be the first time a family's heritage has been explored by the children in it.

Jesus had an extended family, and so do we. Such explorations will enhance our appreciation of our own incarnation and birth. By studying both, a healthy appreciation of our own requirements for strong families and solid communities is fostered. Studies like these make Scripture personal and immediate.

Fourth Sunday (Advent I): Luke 1:26–38. The story of the Annunciation of Mary. The angel Gabriel appears to Mary and tells her she is to bear a son. Gabriel hints at light in the tradition of such prophets as Isaiah.

This Sunday is also the first Sunday following Thanksgiving, and foods can be presented at the altar during the Offertory. Food "lightens" hunger with hope. It is a beautiful way to celebrate Advent.

Also, the first candle in the Advent wreath is lighted.

THE ADVENT WREATH

The modern Advent wreath dates all the way back to Germanic sun-worshiping tribes. Every winter their sun-god, Sol Invictus, seemed to grow weak and come close to death. December 22 is the date of the winter solstice, the day on which the sun reaches the lowest point in its winter path, and the shortest day of the year.

The tribespeople knew that if Sol Invictus died they too would die, victims of freezing cold. Summer crops would never spring afresh. So they wrapped their carts' wheels with evergreen, attached lit candles to them, and hung the wheels from the highest rafters of their meeting halls. The candles, evergreen, and wheels symbolized their hope that Sol Invictus would return again to shed life-giving light and warmth on a cold and dark world.

Several hundred years ago, a few Christians saw a remarkable similarity between this pagan festival and Christmas. They knew Christmas had occurred in late December not because history records it as the date of Jesus' birth but because it was the time of the solstice, when the sun begins its "return" to the world. By hanging brightly wound candle-wheels in their homes, they expressed their conviction that Christ would always come into the world as its true light (Luke 1:78–79).

To these Christians the wheel represented God's eternity—and Alpha (first) and Omega (last) are the symbols of Advent. They covered the wheel with evergreen to symbolize the new life to come. The four purple candles symbolized the ages of "sitting in darkness," awaiting the Christ. The white candle in the middle symbolized God's Christ.

On successive Sundays, more light is added, until at Christmas the wreath blazes. After Christmas the wreath is removed, and a Christ candle burns alone.

Fifth Sunday (Advent 2): Luke 1:39–49. The story of the Visitation of Mary. Mary visits with Elizabeth for three months before the birth of John (St. John the Baptist). Elizabeth greets her guest as the Mother of the Lord, and the Magnificat is introduced. Great things are getting closer. There is more light yet on the Advent wreath.

Sixth Sunday (Advent 3): Luke 1:13–17, 36–37, 57–60, 80. The birth of John the Baptist. Old Zechariah, a priest at the temple in Jerusalem, is told that his wife Elizabeth will bear a son. This story is in the tradition of God's telling Abraham that Sarah will have a child in her old age. The implicit lesson, especially powerful for the early Church, was that as God was faithful to Abraham, the father of the Jewish people, he is just as faithful yet, and for a second time. A child is born, named John, acclaimed holy, a deliverer of the people and forerunner of God's Messiah.

Chrismon Sunday (Advent 4): Luke 2:1–20. Jesus' birth is very near. The light is almost here, and worship concludes the teaching term begun just after All Saints. The fourth candle is lighted, and children hang Chrismons on large Christmas trees in the chancel, perhaps offering them for the tree at the time of their communion. We give, and God gives. It is lovely.

Following the service there is a birthday party for Jesus in the parish hall. For everybody.

ABOUT CHRISMONS

"Why bother to fill time making things when there's so much to be learned during this term?" Two reasons: First, signs and symbols have a way of communicating life's deepest meanings, and second, in our study we share ourselves with one another . . . and fellowship grows.

The term "Chrismon" is derived from "Chris (+) mons." "Monograms of Christ" were first used by early Christians to identify themselves to one another. In many cases, those bearing them were risking exposure, even death.

One of the earliest symbols of the resurrection was the butterfly. The image of a butterfly in flight communicates a feeling of life and freedom; it is a spiritual reality that cannot be expressed in words. Easter eggs are another sign of the resurrection and, though not often used anymore in relation to Easter worship, the hanging of empty, colored eggs on the bare branch of a tree, making an "egg tree," has often symbolized in Easter worship God's promise of life.

To enhance children's appreciation of the significance of signs and symbols, you may want to spend some time exploring ones used today, or those describing the pupils' families. A heart, for instance, symbolizes feelings of love, and a person's initials are closely related to his or her personhood. Books on Christian signs and symbols are readily available.

Chrismons are generally colored gold and white. Gold symbolizes the king's crown Jesus could have rightfully worn but which he disdained in favor of a servant's role. White is the Christian color of celebration, joy, and light.

Chrismons are an essential part of the festival ending the Christmas term. They can be made from dough, styrofoam, beads, paste, or other materials, and hung on large spruce trees flanking the altar.

One Sunday in Advent can be designated a Chrismon day. It can be a grand day for intergenerational learning. Cancel all classroom activity, and gather in the parish hall parents and children of all ages. Then, amidst piles of styrofoam, paste, ribbons, and beads, make Chrismons together, or put together an Advent wreath for home dining tables. Families respond positively to doing projects together.

Classes seem to work best when they have picked just one or two symbols. If the teacher has researched them in advance, it is easy for him or her to share information about the symbols as they are being made concrete. During the Christmas term, those who teach older children may consider volunteering their pupils, on a Sunday or two, as assistant teachers of younger children. The very young need a lot of attention, and while Chrismons are being made, their teachers' hands are full. It is hectic work, and sometimes older children can provide a welcome relief, while learning something about giving, caring, and taking responsibility for others.

THE CHRISMON FESTIVAL: THE TERM CELEBRATES

On the Sunday before Christmas day (the last Sunday of the Advent season) the lesson's focus is always on the birth of Jesus. A pageant is the best of all ways to tell the tale.

Children *and adults* from every grade in the church school are encouraged to take part. Some are the wise, some the shepherds, some the angels. There can be several sheep, a couple of goats, a wooden cow, a live dog, etc. Use your imagination, and have fun.

All classes are preempted by a birthday party for Jesus. One class, or several, can take responsibility for preparing the birthday party in the parish hall. The party itself is a nice gift to give.

CHILDREN'S WORSHIP ON CHRISTMAS DAY

A small but increasing number of parishes are celebrating the holiday by allowing time for the very young to "show" their gifts on Christmas morning or at late afternoon Evening Prayer. One church calls it "The March of the Toys," and another calls it a "Blessing of the Toys." But no matter what it is called, enthusiasm and gratitude abound. You and I both know who is at work in the midst of those feelings.

And because some of the toys will be all too quickly discarded, they might very well next grace the manger at Epiphany.

PLANNING AHEAD FOR EPIPHANY

As the parish anticipates Christmas, remind your pupils—and the adults—to set aside a gift or two for presentation at the celebration of the Epiphany. Though Epiphany occurs on the twelfth day after Christmas, worship on the Sunday nearest is a grand time for opulently dressed wise folk to make their visit. Following in their steps, parishioners can present wrapped toys, leaving them at the manger, to be later presented to the pediatrics unit of a local hospital. Many a nurse will thank you for thinking of their small charges long before the latter were hospitalized. Here, too, is an expression of God's providence, though only the faithful will see it as such.

The necessary reminders can be made throughout Advent. Either especially bought presents or "extras" are appropriate. Our response to the Light of the World is one of rejoicing and, as the darkness of the world is pushed back by God's light, the response of gift-giving is a way to bridge the important terms of Christmas and Epiphany.

SOME SUNDAY-CLASSROOM ACTIVITIES

The following list gives an overview of just a few of the possibilities for Sunday-school education. Perhaps an older class can help a younger one with a project, providing the "light" of help to both children and teachers. Parents can also assist. Community life is enhanced when we learn things together.

Children can help the wider parish family by participating in the Christmas pagent. Pageant participants ought not be limited, however, to children alone; adults, too, should participate, thereby exemplifying the interest and commitment so important for children to see.

FIRST SUNDAY:

—The Christian-education bulletin board on light and darkness ought to be up.
—Who will do a bulletin board in Advent on Jesus' birth? Remember, no news is bad news.
—The Arch Books are big helps with Bible stories.
—Look at the lesson plans suggested in the back of each Arch Book.
—Continue to explore the themes of light and darkness.
—Did you finish all you wanted to do with your saint?
—Can you use your saint to help explain light and darkness?
—Mention the canned goods for the Emergency Food Closet, to be presented in three weeks.
—How about a drama on light and darkness, to be presented to the adult class or other church-school classes?
—What does it feel like to be in the dark?
—Have your pupils imagine what it is like to be hungry.
—Invite them to come to Sunday school next week without breakfast, or to sit in class and just look at a doughnut for a time— how does that feel?

SECOND SUNDAY:

—Remind the children to bring canned goods in two weeks. How is food like "light" to hungry persons?
—Both parents and children should participate in this offering of gifts.
—Why do we offer gifts?
—Think about making Chrismons.
—Who would like to participate in the Christmas pageant?
—Which class will coordinate the birthday party for Jesus?
—What kind of cake will we have?

—How does the food we shall present next week "lighten" empty tummies?

—How about presenting a play, or an art show?

—What does it feel like to be in the dark?

—Can your older class help the younger classes make Chrismons in December?

—A lot is going to be happening between now and then. Only four more Sundays for study.

THIRD SUNDAY:

—Only three more Sundays for study.

—Your class should be beginning to make Chrismons.

—Don't forget to make Chrismons for parents, too. Your pupils can give them as gifts.

—Would your class like to present a drama based on part of the birth narrative?

—Or would your class like to put the whole narrative together into one drama and present it to the adult class or a younger class?

—Make an Advent wreath (or wreaths).

—Prepare the children for the hanging of the great Advent wreath in the church.

—Don't forget to encourage their participation in Thanksgiving worship.

—Food will be presented next week during communion.

THANKSGIVING DAY.

FOURTH SUNDAY:

—The first Sunday in Advent.

—Presentation of food at the parish Eucharist. The legacy of sharing at a time of Thanksgiving goes back a lot further than the early American settlers and the Indians.

In the book of Nehemiah we read: After the Hebrew exiles had returned and rebuilt their homes and walls of Jerusalem, Ezra the priest stood before them and read the Law. And they renewed the covenant. These were their instructions to future generations:

> You may go now; refresh yourselves with rich food and sweet drink, and send a share to all who cannot provide for themselves; for this day is holy to our Lord. Let

there be no sadness, for joy in the Lord is your strength.
[Nehemiah 8:10, The New English Bible]

—Bring your classes by the altar to see how much food was
donated. Everyone working together makes a difference.
—Anyone interested in packing the food in boxes (and providing
the boxes, too!)?
—The Advent wreath is hung and lighted.
—The birth narrative is beginning. How are you using it?
—Can older children help younger ones with their work?
—What about your participation in the Christmas pageant?
—Can you use the choir and the organist to teach Christmas
hymns?
—Discuss the hymns.
—Draw pictures of Jesus' family, and discuss the story.
—Have your children bring pictures of their families, immediate
and extended.
—How are their families like Jesus' family?
—Make a papier-mâché crèche.
—Look for the church's crèche in the nave of the church.
—With your children, wonder what the Chrismon trees will look
like after they are decorated on the Sunday before Christmas.
—Can the older classes present a drama to the younger classes?
—Could a younger class present a drama to an older class or the
adult class?
—Look at the ideas on the back pages of the Arch Books.

FIFTH SUNDAY:
—Second Sunday in Advent.
—Two candles are lighted in the wreath.
—What does that mean?
—How is your Advent wreath coming?
—Mention family participation in the decoration of the church
(e.g., hanging the greens just before Christmas).
—Will someone help get the Christmas trees?
—Wonder how many we shall need.
—Pageant practice will begin.
—Learn Christmas hymns.
—Discuss them.
—Are you using the Bible stories?
—Remind children of the "extra" gift to be presented at Epiph-
any on the first Sunday of the new year.

—Teach about our giving to others because God gives to us.
—What does God give?
—Talk about the light of God's love moving into the world.
—Have you invited parents to your class to help with Chrismons?
—Have your pupils remembered to make some for their parents?

SIXTH SUNDAY:

—Third Sunday in Advent.
—Finished your Chrismons?
—Final touches on the pageant will be made.
—Encourage your pupils and their parents to help prepare the Christmas decorations for the church.
—Remind the children of the Epiphany present for the hospital.
—Continue to develop God's light.
—Look for the Christ candle to appear—it's in the middle of the Advent wreath.
—Do you know when it will be lighted?
—Why will it be lighted?
—How are your Bible stories coming?

SEVENTH SUNDAY:

—The Chrismon Festival and birthday party for Jesus.
—The pageant is presented.
—The Chrismon trees decorated.
—The term is too quickly over—and it seems just to have begun.

CHRISTMAS EVE AND DAY.

Note

1. Lesson plan courtesy of Martha Pollie Lenz, then new at teaching, and planning carefully.

CHAPTER ELEVEN

The Epiphany Term: Light for the World

NO POST-CHRISTMAS LETDOWN

"Light for the World" is a capsule description of Epiphany's theme. Everything revolves around it and, as in the other terms, more material is available than you can possibly use.

Epiphany's opening worship moves the attitude of Christmas to the new calendar year and sounds a joyful note for studies in the winter months that follow.

There is no post-Christmas educational letdown.

Teaching teams must set close and realistic limits on the subjects they intend to teach. Remember, with just a few minutes available on Sunday morning, less is often more. The adage introduced in chapter 5 offers encouragement:

I hear and I forget.

I see and I remember.

I do and I understand.

Wander through the following pages freely. Then plan the six or seven weeks of the term. Keep things simple.

Class projects can center on such things as:

—short plays about Jesus' life and ministry,
—your parish's current ministry or history, or
—deepening children's appreciation of their participation in Holy Communion.

EPIPHANY'S CATHEDRAL WORSHIP

Epiphany and Easter/Pentecost are the only two terms that begin with cathedral worship. Both are responses to the coming of Christ: Easter/Pentecost begins at the point of resurrection; Epiphany begins because Jesus has come to the world.

1. Near the beginning of the term, on a Sunday near the twelfth day of Christmas—the traditional time of the visit of the Three Kings—parishioners may offer gifts to the Christ child. This drama is an extension of the Christmas pageant.

Because of this, local hospital patients may be enriched with gifts. The donated presents might be extra ones from Christmas, or duplicates, or ones bought especially for the occasion. Pediatric units often need all the help they can get in providing emotional care for sick youngsters, especially those hospitalized for lengthy periods.

God's ministry to his world is well supported by our care. You may call it "Christmas outreach"; it is social action at its best.

The day's worship can be shaped this way: I have seen congregations divided into three sections so that each can follow a king as they present their gifts at the altar. I have also seen the Three Kings dramatically proceed at the time of the Offertory, each singing solo a verse from "We Three Kings,"[1] the congregation later offering their gifts at the rail during communion. God feeds directly, and through our love God also feeds the world.

2. On the evening of the twelfth day of Christmas, or the Sunday nearest January sixth, whichever is most convenient, the choir and congregation can celebrate a Feast of Lights. It is a dramatic evening worship. Lavishly dressed kings may again present their gifts, one of which can be a smoking pot of incense, at the altar. After congregational singing of some of the most familiar carols, light—in the now-darkened church—is passed from the Christ Candle near the altar, hand to hand, to candles held by everyone. The hushed darkness makes the source of light all the more vivid. In a blaze of candleglow, the liturgy ends with a great procession to some of the most joyous of Christmas music.

A parish-hall party is a good way to end this altogether beautiful event. Here is Christian education at its best.

3. A "See and Believe" festival ends the term's learning. It is a grand time to celebrate the world's positive response to God's light of Jesus.

"See and Believe" takes its cue from the story of the Transfiguration (Matthew 17:2, Mark 9:2), which is appointed by almost every worship lectionary to be read on the Sunday before Lent. The Transfiguration marks the day the disciples saw Jesus in conversation with Moses (the Law) and Elijah (the Prophet), and seeing, believed. Here is Epiphany's theme: Seeing the light of God's Christ, we believe God loves us.

The "See and Believe Festival" also picks up the joyous note of Shrove Tuesday, two days later.

The day's worship might include banners displaying that which the children have studied in the classroom, maybe even a grandly constructed chancel drama of one of Jesus' healings.

If the Bishop's schedule allows, this term is a good time for confirmation. The festival can easily include those about to be confirmed—and the Bishop will probably enjoy the party as well. Even if confirmation is impossible, some people may want to reaffirm their baptismal vows, and others, to renew their commitment to Christian service.[2]

ON THE TEACHING USE OF CANDLES AND LIGHT
IN THE CHURCH YEAR

Candles and their light are special to Christians. They always have been.

At the very outset of the Christian year the Advent wreath is shown. It celebrates God's promise of light and life. After Christmas the four purple candles give way to the splendor of one large, bright white candle. (The wreath itself is removed until next Advent.) The Christ Candle lights every candle of the parish at Epiphany, and it remains in place near the Baptismal Font until Holy Week. On Maundy Thursday the light of God's Christ is extinguished and the church stripped of all color.

On the day of the Resurrection, flanked by lighted torches in grand procession, the Christ candle repossesses the church. There it remains until a Sunday near the Ascension, when it is removed until next Advent.

Candles on the altar suffice to remind the Church of God's light during the season of Pentecost, which runs from the first weeks of June through November. Then the Advent wreath reappears, and the cycle begins again.

Candles are highly visual teaching aids. They touch the simple curiosity in all of us. Happily, God uses them to help us readily and gently strike a relationship with his light for the world.

EIGHT TOPICS FOR STUDY

The themes of All Saints and Christmas lead right into Epiphany.

The "special persons" focus of All Saints prepares for the special person of Jesus, and the theme of light in the Christmas term moves us right into an exploration of the Light of the World.

All this makes Epiphany one of the most important terms. All Saints and Christmas, necessary as they are, stimulate us all to wonder and explore in the direction of Jesus Christ and his Church. They do the advance work necessary for good Epiphany study.

TOPIC ONE: JESUS GROWING UP—A JEWISH CHILDHOOD

Jesus is light. One option for study is to trace Jesus' life and Jewish heritage as he grew into adulthood.

The Gospels provide more material than many realize, and it is especially effective when correlated with the growing up our pupils are doing. Eight stories follow.

1. Each Christmas Jesus' birth warms the hearts of millions of Christians, and millions of us through the ages have responded just like the Wise of old, with gifts.

This story is probably the one all of us know best, and it is the subject of almost every Christmas pageant.

2. But tragedy was also occasioned by Jesus' birth. Though it is often glossed over, not everyone was glad Jesus was born.

Herod, angered that another might challenge his crown and hoping to put the threat away, slaughtered the children in Jesus' neighborhood. The slaughter of the Innocents (Matthew 2:1–17) is marked by a holy day right after Christmas Day.

Innocent persons suffer senselessly in life; it is an irrefutable fact. We Christians call it the consequence of a deep and tragic flaw, our sinfulness. The Church, without trying to rationalize it away, simply affirms a tragic reality beyond understanding. The opening page of the Epiphany term also hints at that which will be spelled out more fully during the time of Lent.

I have spent more than a few class sessions with young children, exploring how scared and insecure Herod must have been, and how grievously sad the innocent children's deaths were for their parents and for God.

(For several weeks after meeting a third-grade class, I also explored an eight-year-old's impression that it would be better "to be dead than not wanted." I heard him speak of himself, and he began to discover in the course of our conversation that he *did* count for me. His other teachers also began to take more interest in his life. Christian education, healing, and wholeness occur, sometimes, in the most unexpected of places. God is good.)

Two days before we remember the deaths of the innocent children, we recall the death of St. Stephen (Acts 6:8–7:2, 51–60), the first Christian martyr.

Jesus' life, lamentably, evoked resentment as well as joy.

3. In the custom of the Jews, at eight days old Jesus was taken to the Temple for circumcision (Luke 2:21–24). It was his rite of initiation into the Jewish community, much as infant baptism is God's way of making a person part of Christ's body. An elderly couple named Simeon and Anna were present. St. Luke understands them to represent Judaism. Convinced they had finally seen God's Christ, Simeon composed a song of thanksgiving (Luke 2:29–32).[3]

4. Matthew chronicles Mary and Joseph's flight to Egypt to avoid Herod's wrath. In their journey to a land in which Jesus' forebears had served as slaves (Genesis 37–Exodus 14), he sees the clear message for the Jewish reader as one of God's deliverance and saving love coming a second time, but this time through his Christ (Matthew 2:12–33).

5. Later the three returned to Nazareth. There Jesus grew into adulthood. Joseph was a carpenter, and Jesus, with younger brothers and sisters, must have played often in the shop, learning the father's trade. This relationship was undoubtedly warm, reflected, at least in part, in Jesus later calling the God of Abraham, Isaac, and Jacob *Abba*, meaning "Poppa."

6. Each year Jesus may have joined his parents in a trip to Jerusalem for Passover. Passover is the Jewish celebration of deliverance from the Egyptian pharaohs, in remembrance of the time God passed over the Jewish homes and slew the first-born of the Egyptian oppressors (Exodus 11).

On one visit Jesus was so caught up in discussions in the Temple that he failed to rejoin his parents for the journey home. (Twelve-year-old children do that yet, causing just as much anguish for today's parents.) You might choose to explore Jesus' behavior or his parents' fears—and how some things never change.

Better, you might investigate the plagues and other events surrounding the Passover (Exodus 7:26–15:19). Jesus would have learned these same stories as a child, and he'd have been fascinated and frightened by God's saving power and careful love.

In this same context, older classes can study Judaism in some detail, perhaps scheduling a Sunday (or other day) on which to visit a Temple.

7. Jesus would have been familiar not only with the Passover story but with the rest of the Old Testament. He was an Israelite, and he well knew the record of events in which the God of History met his people. Stories from the Torah (i.e., the Pentateuch) would have been as familiar to Jesus, for instance, as his prayer is to us. The Ten Commandments (Exodus 20) were certainly part of his education, and he was doubtless familiar with the Twenty-third Psalm.

Like Jesus' parents and teachers, you might like to consider assigning some memory work to your class. The chapter titled *Imaginative Bible Study* has more on this topic.

8. Nothing more is known about Jesus' growing up until the time of John the Baptist (Matthew 3:1–22).

Jesus was baptized by John, and the Spirit descended with the words, "This is my son, my beloved" (Matthew 3:13–17). Acknowledged as God's Christ, Jesus began his ministry in earnest.

TOPIC TWO: TELLING THE GOOD NEWS ABOUT JESUS

The word "gospel" means "good news." The good news is: We are made by God for life, health, and wholeness; we are not made for death. In Jesus' life, death, and resurrection, the world began to glimpse God's promise of life for us all.

That is this section's great theme. In addition to that which follows, still more help is to be found in Easter/Pentecost's studies of St. Paul and Jesus. In fact, Paul was without equal when it came to telling the good news about Jesus. How do I know? The formation of the Christian Church is proof.

THE SHAPE OF GOOD NEWS

What does good news feel like? I can provide a few clues, but the work of identifying the feeling will have to be your own. If you are able to work through this process for yourself, you will be able more effectively to lead your pupils down the same path.

A gospel feeling is what we get after we close our eyes for a long period of time, feel the impotence of being unable to see, and then open our eyes again to the world about us. It is the good-news feeling one gets after having hobbled about on a crutch and then finding it "really can" be put away. It is the feeling that emerges as one hears the words "Well done" after one has completed a very difficult task (Matthew 25:21, 23). It has to do with being noticed and set free, and the resultant satisfaction, peace, acceptance, and enthusiasm.

The following biblical stories illustrate this feeling. Wonder about how the people in them felt as they experienced gospel for themselves, and as you do so in your class, the same feeling will be present today, nineteen hundred years later.

1. Blind Bartimaeus (Mark 10:46–52), a pushy man, got what he wanted, his sight, because he asked for it. How did his long-closed eyes feel when they saw the face of the man who gave them sight? That is a gospel feeling.

2. I wonder how the lame man felt as his friends gathered him up on a bed, took him to a house in which Jesus met with others, only to discover they could not move near the one who might help (Luke 5:18–26). That is bad news, like hell.

I wonder how his feelings changed when those same friends discovered the outside staircase to the roof. But I wonder most what he felt when he heard the words, "Rise . . . and walk." That is gospel.

3. Wonder with your pupils how Jairus—a strong, important, and highly respected Roman soldier—felt, knowing his small daughter was dying (Luke 8:40–42, 49–56)?

And then I wonder about the change in his feelings when he heard she was alive again.

So tell good news to your class. The Arch Books are a helpful source, and lots of other commercial materials are readily available. The fact is, however, this: your imagination and the Bible stories are not only the cheapest way to go but the best. This book's chapter, *Imaginative Bible Study* and the Easter/Pentecost and All-Saints terms—in that order—offer made-to-order help as well.

THE CLASSROOM ATMOSPHERE FOR LEARNING: Work to create in your classroom an atmosphere in which your students can begin to feel gospel for themselves. The Church has not grown because it had to but because our happy response to God's good news simply cannot be contained.

THE BOTTOM LINE: The more you use the great stories of God's presence and ministry, the more you hasten the birth of natural and Christian faith, and the more your students will be able to discern for themselves God's good-news presence and ministry today.

TOPIC THREE: THE LIFE YOUR PARISH BRINGS TO GOD'S WORLD

We are made for relationships. Many of us find in our Churches the support and encouragement we need to enjoy life as fully as possible. In many ways good news is a parish community of care and affectionate relationships.

We don't come together as a community of faith because we alone chose it; we come together because God first calls and we decide to respond. Nor do we have to go to church to be Christian, but most Christians cannot help but do so. Family ties are like that.

Help your children consider the community of relationships we call Church.

1. Your parish church consists of all sorts of people. Encourage your children to look around and notice them.

An adult acolyte, seated behind the rail during the time of communion, was once struck with the varieties of hands stretching outward. Some were tiny and fresh, others gnarled, but all were reaching. "When two or three are gathered in my name . . ." (Matthew 18:20) is the promise.

Wonder with your pupils about who the two or three are, and help the former open their eyes to the world in which they live.

Why do these folks attend? Are other members of their families present? What are their ages? How do they earn their living? And how do they help God take care of his world (a note first played during the All-Saints term)?

Invite a few of these people to come and explain why the Church is part of their lives.

2. Your class is a small community. Work at raising its collective consciousness about those persons important in the pupils' immediate lives—parents, peers, friends, and so on.

How are the latter light for the world of your pupil? What is the content of their light? Is it security, a good meal, a warm place to call home, an exciting ball game, a happy conversation?

One hymn puts it this way: "In Christ there is no east or west, in Him no south or north."[4] In the community of your class you may want to explore who forms "the east" and who "the west."

Your pupils may come from many places, and you will be doing them a favor by sensitizing them to their differences while stressing that we are all, nevertheless, part of a single body.

3. Or you may want to explore the ministries of those parishioners who help you function as a church family: acolytes, custodians, lay readers, chalice bearers, organists, choirs, church-school teachers, clergy, altar-guild members, vestry or board members, wardens, and the office staff. Each helps sustain the communion you share as a community of the faithful.

We are nourished by the healthy feelings of a well-established and cohesive family life. Take them away or discourage their development, and the body is impoverished.

Schedule visits by some of the persons listed above. Ask them to take your class "on tour," explaining their work as they go. They will probably be honored you asked, and your class will be impressed that these persons cared enough to participate.

4. One year an eighth-grade class took an armload of books on Christian symbolism and walked around the church, identifying symbols as they went. Some stood in the pulpit and behind the Lord's Table, and they ended up asking questions they had wondered about for years. Others took pleasure in identifying the symbols they had seen presented in Chrismons. Children are naturally curious.

5. Another class might be interested in creating a slide show about parish life or about what the parishioners do in the world, in their everyday work-for-pay jobs. Who doesn't like to see his or her neighbors on the screen?

TOPIC FOUR: EXPLORING YOUR CHURCH'S HISTORY

The history of your parish is a gift that confers a vision of God's action over the years, each generation giving way to the next.

I am saddened at how infrequently we encourage this kind of retrospection, the lack of which results in a people cut off from their history and roots, who, though alive in the moment, are impoverished by understanding little of God's mighty action in bringing them to the present.

Your class may decide to sponsor a parish homecoming, for God uses such events to let his people know that "before you were formed in the womb I knew you . . ." (Jeremiah 1:4).

Better, ask older parishioners to tell the parish story as best they remember it. They will probably refer to issues important a generation ago, and with just a bit of Bible-imaginative speculation, you will be able to see the way God moved in your congregation's midst in days long past. Through these elder eyes a new generation of Christians will more deeply engage current parish life, perhaps glimpsing a bit more fully God's hand at work in the world.

To interpret the story as I suggest means risking declarations about God's presence and ministry, but it is a method by which the eyes of the blind are opened and the ears of the deaf unstopped.

It is God who calls a people together. Though his mighty acts today may not compare with the spectacle of a pillar of cloud by day and a pillar of fire by night (Exodus 13:21, 14:19, 24), the fact is, by recalling our past, we root the present more firmly. The same dreams that empowered the past also forge enthusiasm today.

TOPIC FIVE: AN EXPLORATION OF BAPTISM

All of us want to feel clean. You know as well as I the dirty feelings occasioned by a harsh word too hastily said and the cleansing effect of an apology.

The word "baptize" means, in Greek, "to wash clean."

Once upon a time an adult class member, when asked, "volunteered" to smear his face with a brown dirt paste we had concocted. Then the whole class reflected on his dirtying himself and easily identified with his unclean feelings. Everyone entered in, we had good fun, and later we all rejoiced with the volunteer in the baptized feeling of being washed clean by warm water.

Here is a good-news feeling. Later, this adult (with several friends) took the skit "on tour" to the lower grades. As I heard it later, there were great fun and lots of learning everywhere they played.

Here is, too, an example of experiential education at its best.

You might also ask your pupils to bring photographs of their baptismal days and help them re-create the times most of them cannot, because of their age, remember. Such assignments also involve the parents at home, and each child can be encouraged to present his or her "day past" in today's classroom.

If you are fortunate enough to discover children who have not yet been baptized and want to be, there is a goldmine, for the entire class will relive their own stories while celebrating the new story taking shape.

If baptism is incorporated into the Epiphany festival, children can be invited to stand near the font, where the act of baptism is most clearly visible.

Coupling this term's studies with the immediacy of the baptismal event communicates a powerful message of God's love. Children may not understand it all, but in their rapt attention and wide-eyed response God touches them at levels of which we are not even aware.

TOPIC SIX: CHILDREN, GOD'S PRESENCE, AND COMMUNION

It is hard to say if we are ever too young to learn. It is harder still to describe God's participation in the learning processes. Nevertheless, we do learn and God participates, and Eucharistic worship for the young child is a powerful educational medium. This theme is discussed in the chapter titled *Parish Worship: A Means of Grace.* Still, a note about it is appropriate here.

If you are using seasonal themes in parish Christian education and everyone is working in the same context, you may be able to schedule, with clergy interest and support, instructed worship.

To provide simple teaching for the very young, a more personal and informal classroom communion, using crackers and juice, may be celebrated. Lay leaders and readers may help: they may vest if that seems appropriate.

Also, families can work on this at home, using some of the suggestions about family worship found in the chapter *Parish Worship: A Means of Grace.*

TOPIC SEVEN: OUR DENOMINATION'S HERITAGE

"In the Bleak Mid-winter" is a lovely hymn.[5] It accurately describes January, February, and March, and it encourages us to look back at some of the things that happened during the fall of the year.

Everyone was "up" in the fall. All kinds of new beginnings were taking place—at home, in church, in the secular community, and in the national consciousness. Some new parishioners may have joined us for the first time. By now, many of them are happily a part of parish life, but others may be still finding their way.

The time after Christmas can be a time to stop and take a closer look at our lives and pilgrimage and maybe to inquire more deeply into the history of the denomination our parish calls home.

The Epiphany term is an excellent time to honor that which has begun to develop in people's lives in the fall. Programs like these honor God's work of bonding his people more closely to himself.

TOPIC EIGHT: ST. PAUL

Paul is one of the great personalities of the Bible. His theology and ministry profoundly shaped the Christian Church. But he too often gets a bad press, mainly because of the doctrinaire approach all too evident in his letters.

The letters were meant to furnish guidance and support. Because Paul often wrote to remote, troubled congregations very new to the faith, he had to apply as much of his authority as possible, simply to impose the order the recipients so desperately needed.

I doubt Paul ever won anyone to Christ by being doctrinaire; because he *did* win many, however, he *must* have been more charismatic than he appears in the Epistles. His mission to Athens (Acts 17:15f), discussed in the chapter *Faith's Birth and Christian Education,* encourages me to think so.

When ought we to study Paul and, through him, allow God to touch our lives? There is already too much material to study in this term, but Epiphany encourages us to think about Paul, mainly because he so happily presented the light of Christ to the world. Further, his feast day falls every year on January 25.

We may do better, however, to explore Paul's life and ministry in the Easter/Pentecost term. Paul's pentecost on the road to Damascus shines like a bright light in the New Testament, and therefore the study of his ministry in the light of Easter's resurrection makes a lot of sense. Accordingly, studies of Paul are suggested under that term's description.

Unfortunately, the Easter/Pentecost term falls at a time of year when, because flowers are budding and the weather is warming, it is hard to hold the class's attention. So the study of Paul suffers.

The All-Saints term is a good setting, and you may choose to place Paul's ministry there.

When all is said and done, the season of Epiphany is a setting Paul would be glad to call home.

SOME SUNDAY-CLASSROOM ACTIVITIES

The suggestions below point to the numerous possibilities for study during this term. They will have served their function if they jog your imagination about those best fitting your schedule.

Remember the Sunday of "See and Believe." Every term-ending festival depends on bright, widespread class participation; your preparations will, in part, dictate its shape. Will there be one big chancel drama—like the Christmas pageant—or several skits, or banners, or more?

Preparations for the festival will consume some of your classroom time and give your teaching sharp focus.

Challenges are always fun, especially when the results are later to be presented to folks who care—in this case, the entire parish.

FIRST SUNDAY:

—Do you know your pupils? Relationships are important.
—Decide which of the themes you will use, and look for the pertinent Arch Bible Books. (The latter are good both for teachers and students.)
—Stop by the altar and look at the presents given in the Epiphany celebration.
—Explore how these presents will enhance the community of the pediatric unit.
—Would your class like to take the gifts to the hospital?
—Begin to think about exploring the relationships in your church community.
—How about an exploration of parish history?
—Encourage your pupils to come to next week's evening Feast of Lights.
—Will your class learn the Twenty-third Psalm or some other?

SECOND SUNDAY:

—Remind your children of the evening Feast of Lights.
—Think about what you intend to present at the term's closing festival, a day for "See and Believe."
—Compare Jesus growing up with the way your children are growing up.
—What did he do and what do your children do as they grow?
—Prepare for the instructed Eucharists; they will add to your classroom activity.
—What kind of instruction would you like in the liturgy?
—Explore the Bible stories.
—Older classes may present a play for a younger class.
—How about a play for the adult class?
—Encourage your children to think about ushering in church.
—Would your children like to learn to be acolytes?
—Bake some bread and eat it while discussing how bread can form a community.
—Think about baptism and what it means to be washed clean.
—How are we dirty?
—How about memorizing a biblical verse?

THIRD SUNDAY:

—What will your class present on "See and Believe" Sunday?
—Do your children remember their baptisms?
—Are there photos?
—Are there any children in your class who might like to be baptized?
—Who are they?
—Let the clergy know.
—What drama can be presented?
—How can the instructed liturgy assist you?
—Take the children to church and let them handle the chalice. Let them practice drinking from it. Ask the Altar Guild to assist you.
—Have your children show pictures about where and how they grew up.
—Have you thought about how the clergy might participate in your teaching?
—How about developing a slide or picture show on your parish's life?

—How about using the lay readers to explain why their task is important to them?

—Have you thought about learning some hymns together?

FOURTH SUNDAY:

—Explore the Bible stories of Jesus growing up.

—Explore the early development of your parish.

—Tour your church building.

—Invite a member of your vestry or board to talk about the parish.

—The Altar Guild can show you how the altar and the table are set up for the Eucharist.

—Let your children explore the sanctuary and the nave.

—May your children practice with the chalice?

—Young children might be taught to stand for communion (which makes it easier for them).

—Ask your children to invite their parents to the classroom Eucharists.

—Share an explanation of your classroom Eucharist when you invite parents.

—Have you used the organist this term?

—Can the choir present a short concert?

—Maybe its members would join in singing in parts, instructing you in harmony.

—They might include your children in the singing.

—They might be pleased to be asked.

FIFTH SUNDAY:

—Look for the Christ Candle that lighted the candles in the Feast of Lights.

—Why was the Advent wreath taken away?

—How about scheduling a practice baptism for your class?

—"Wash the children clean," and discuss being dirty.

—Help connect being washed clean with the confession of saying, "I'm sorry."

—Discuss standing to receive at communion when we feel joyful.

—Discuss kneeling to receive communion when we feel especially penitential.

—Do you have any children who want to be baptized?

—Which class might like to host the term-ending parish reception?

Sixth Sunday:

—Explore the biblical stories suggested above.
—We need a Christian-education bulletin board for Lent.
—Together, bake some bread in the parish kitchen.
—Then discuss how the Christian family forms around eating and drinking together.
—Where did it all begin?
—Teach the children how to receive communion.
—Help the children describe what they see at communion—who is there?—and what feelings do they pick up?

Seventh Sunday:

—Continue to explore biblical stories.
—Explore how we feel after sharing food together.
—What color is this feeling?
—That color is the feeling of communion for your children.
—Use the parish kitchen for baking.
—What is the "body" of your class like?
—How do its members differ?
—How are they alike?

Eighth Sunday:

—What are some of the Christian symbols used in the church?
—Why not have a "search party" look around?
—Which ones were used for Chrismons?
—Have you looked recently at the All-Saints banners?
—Who are they of? How are they "light" for Epiphany?
—Encourage participation in next Sunday's "See and Believe" festival.

Last Sunday:

—The "See and Believe" festival.
—A party follows.
—Are you ready now for Shrove Tuesday? And pancakes?

Notes

1. *The Hymnal of the Protestant Episcopal Church, 1940* (New York: The Church Pension Fund, 1940), Hymn 51.

2. *The Book of Common Prayer, 1979.* "The Reaffirmation of Baptismal Vows," p. 419, and "A Form of Commitment to Christian Service," p. 420.

3. Ibid., 120.

4. *The Hymnal of the Protestant Episcopal Church, 1940,* Hymn 263.

5. Ibid., Hymn 44.

CHAPTER TWELVE

The Lenten Term: This Is My Son, My Beloved

DARKNESS, HURT, AND INJUSTICE

Darkness is in the world, and people hurt. As we struggle to make sense of the more painful side of living, Lent is a counterpoint to Epiphany.

Generations of Christians have wondered and yearned to know how God is present (even *if* he is present) in life's most abject times. Honest questions deserve honest and sensitive treatment, and Lent is the best time to do so.

God is, of course, present at *all* times, but the pain of the moment tends to blind us to it. Many of us, looking for the fresh breeze of his spirit bringing life, are mostly unprepared for the experience of suffering and death; at the least, it is a reality we would rather avoid. We can, however, prepare ourselves for it, and the season of Lent has always been the season devoted to this end.

THE LENTEN TERM

The Lenten term takes its cue from Maundy Thursday and Good Friday. By expanding their focus to include all six weeks, Lent provides an opportunity for us to explore God's promise of life even in the midst of suffering.

THE POINT OF THE TERM IS: The Easter cross, fixed at the end of the term, is like a beacon, a steady promise, an assurance of hope. Good Friday may be a day of death, but it is good because God took the worst of life and made it new.

By weaving explorations around this theme throughout the term, class activity can be the avenue through which the reality of God's love becomes apparent, not because answers are given but because the close connections between life and death are directly related to his care for us all.

Many teachers might prefer to hedge a bit in these studies, recognizing that there are few answers to pain and hurt; they simply are. Nevertheless, there *are* some answers that make a lot of sense, and careful inquiry satisfies hard questions honestly asked.

Rich materials present themselves for this term's study, and this chapter only scratches their surface. Since there are only six Sundays with which to work, plan carefully.

MAKING USE OF WORSHIP

This term's worship actually begins with the *Shrove Tuesday Pancake Supper.* Because many Christians once fasted during the forty days of Lent, the days immediately before were treated as the last chance for a party. The annual New Orleans Mardi Gras is one expression of this practice—and pancakes, sausages, and syrup are another (albeit more moderate).

On *Ash Wednesday* evening, the very next night, Lent's note of passion is struck. Because it occurs at night and at midweek, families seldom attend church together. That is a mistake, for with even a modicum of parental commitment to the joint learning process, children as young as five or six can sense something is in the air. Their involvement, this early in the term, naturally prepares for the reading of the Passion Gospel on Palm Sunday, and the liturgy of death, still later, on Maundy Thursday evening.

At midterm, to deepen studies of death and dying, an especially instructed *Burial Office* can be incorporated into Sunday morning's worship. By itself, or with the Eucharist and a selection of triumphant hymns (perhaps with brass accompaniment), the worship can be instructive. The community of faith, though loving life, does not deny the reality of death, nor of pain and suffering. Nor is death explained away; it simply is, to be redeemed.

Since every class is exploring the impassioned side of life, the

Burial Office encourages them to probe more deeply into the boundaries of our existence.

Christians in increasing numbers appear to shy away from a church service for the burial of a family member. Among other reasons, it may be that the building is too large or the arrangement of an unfamiliar service too complex.

But these circumstances did not always apply. Several hundred years ago community life centered around church activity. In recent years, as funeral homes have extended more comprehensive services, Christians seem to be taking less frequent advantage of church worship as a way to deal with these tender times.

There is an alternative. The Burial Office, said in church (with hymns and, perhaps, the celebration of the Eucharist) is both good pastoral care and good education.

The fourth Sunday of Lent lends itself to an instructed Burial Office. Ever since medieval times, this Sunday has been viewed as a pause in Lent's austerity, a day to remind ourselves that the purpose of Lent is ultimately not our sorrow for sins but preparation for the glory revealed in the cross and the resurrection.

Facing squarely the worst of life, we find God's loving presence there as well.

Palm Sunday can be, with just a little care, teaching at its best. Following the blessing of palms and the palms scattering among the congregation, the Great Procession may begin with "All Glory, Laud and Honor."[1] The bright atmosphere is set for Jesus' triumphant entry into Jerusalem.

The Eucharist builds on this festive note—but never far in the background is the shadow of the impending Passion. Following communion, the events of the Passion Gospel might be read as a second gospel. Designated readers, each taking a part, debate Jesus' life, and the congregation becomes the frenzied crowd demanding his blood. Worship might end with the final amen of "Ah, Holy Jesus, How Hast Thou Offended."[2] In that moment, left empty, the gathered community is brought right up against the moment of Jesus' despair.

But why leave this great gospel until the end? The inclusion of children means we have to pay as much attention to their needs as we do to everyone else's; fair is fair.

This pattern is also much more sensible. If a great procession of palms shapes the first part of worship, children have something to hang onto until the second act—the Holy Communion—and they are all ears when the Passion Gospel is finally read. By it all of us are propelled into Maundy Thursday's drama. I have found that this service, constructed this way, almost guarantees the attendance of children and parents on Thursday night.

The mood of passion deepens on the evening of *Maundy Thursday.* The day takes its name from an earlier designation—Commandment Thursday. On the night of the Last Supper Jesus said to his disciples, "A new commandment I give to you, that you love one another." Careless enunciation by the medieval English accounts for the change.

The early Christians, whether Jew or Gentile, enslaved or free, rich or poor, came together on this special evening for an *agape* meal, or love feast, in many places. We celebrate Maundy or Commandment Thursday the same way yet.

A Maundy Thursday Eucharist can recall the Lord's Last Supper. Following communion, the interior of the church is stripped of hangings and brass. All ornaments giving color and vitality to the scene are removed. As lights in the church are extinguished or slowly dimmed, the bare altar is washed clean. Those who assisted in the removals return to their seats, the cross is draped, and the gathered community leaves in silence. It is, as best it can be made, an expression of death. The Christ Candle stands solitary and alone, its flame, too, extinguished.

Easter morning rings in with a Grand Procession. The impoverished altar is vested and the shiny silver used for communion processed. A brass choir might accompany the singing of hymns, and during the time of communion a large cross may be adorned with the blossoms of springtime's gardens and fields. Lent's pilgrimage is over.

Christian education takes place best in an atmosphere of curious exploration, and learning is considerably enhanced by the parish at worship.

As the congregation is apprised of developing plans, every age group and family unit is included in something larger than itself. More participation means increased enthusiasm, and the term becomes the kind of celebration only God can make.

SHAPING LESSON PLANS

Read through the following materials with yourself in mind. Some teachers may want to explore death and dying for the whole six weeks, others may choose to touch on it only now and again, preferring to explore the "risky" ministry of Jesus, or the suffering of those who, Church history remembers, dared to care.

The stations of the cross were explored by a class during one Lenten term.

Though this part of our Christian heritage is used mostly in the Roman Catholic tradition, a third-grade class, depending on their teacher's interest and enthusiasm, learned the tortured events of Jesus' last days through the pilgrimage she led.

The stations were painted, modeled in clay, and illustrated with simple drawings. As each project was finished, it was displayed in the church. Thus the whole parish learned right along with the children.

For six weeks the class was able to explore the theme of death in a simple way, always based on walking with Jesus.

What made this teaching so good? The imagination and commitment of this third-grade teacher, and her desire to involve her students.

She also made good use of the adage introduced in chapter 5:

I hear and I forget.

I see and I remember.

I do and I understand.

The teacher's imagination is always an important key to success in the classroom.

There are only a few weeks in which to work, and, considering that the last two may be devoted fully to Jesus' passion, time must be carefully planned.

For those classes wanting to explore the theme of death, Sunday's worship can provide added support. Class discussions of funerals and *The Book of Common Prayer*'s "Ministration at the Time of Death" can be enlightening. Clergy are well prepared to help with them.

Children are keenly curious about events surrounding death; in fact, they are more open to them than many adults. Death seems more threatening the older we become, though I have found that when children's visits to a funeral home are scheduled, we never lack for parental sponsors who want to come along "just to see." For more than a few adults, such a visit has made preparations for later funerals easier than they would have been otherwise.

EXPLORING LIFE AND DEATH: MAKING USE OF ST. STEPHEN

Death and dying may seem like overwhelming issues, but both are easily explored by means of story. The Bible is full of stories of persons who lived and died; every story is waiting to be used, and many are already familiar.

St. Stephen's martyrdom (Acts 5–8) provides a context in which death can be gently engaged. Beginning in the fifth chapter, the author of Acts—probably the Luke who wrote the gospel—notes that as the gospel spread, some of Israel's priests began to fear it. (Peter had already encountered some hostility.)

Stephen was a Jew, and Temple authorities were prepared to make him an example for others who might be considering desertion, as they saw it, from Jewish heritage.

Stephen's self-defense is recorded in Acts, chapter 7. This brief section is also a bright and concise summary of Jewish history.

Stephen defended himself by appealing to his tradition and showing how Jesus was the one for whom Israel had long hoped. He was, however, found guilty and was later stoned. A man called Saul stood by, watching, and though we know him better as St. Paul, his memory of this first Christian's martyrdom probably had a substantial impact on his later conversion.

You may wonder with your children what Stephen might have felt as the rocks were thrown at him. Or you may re-create the scene, using wads of paper for rocks; but if you do, for the very young please have Jesus come and stop the stoning before St. Stephen dies.

No matter what you do, always take time afterward to reflect on it, by asking your children what they saw and felt. This is what will happen: They will teach you how it would have been for them. That is how true identification takes place. Was Stephen scared? Where did he find the courage to face it?

Stephen's death is remembered every year on December 26. Though often overlooked because of Christmas Day's immediacy, the reminder is clear: The birth of God's Christ brings not only joy, like that of hearing angels singing, but death.

EXPLORING LIFE AND DEATH: TEN OTHER WAYS

1. *Jesus' death* will shortly be upon us. Explore the story, maybe building studies around classroom drama based on Luke (Lk. 23:33f). Present the play to other classes, or to a group of parents or the adult class.

A few weeks ago Jesus' Christmas birth was celebrated. In this compressed period our pupils will sense that it is simply "wrong" for this child-now-man to die.

2. If your church has *stained glass windows* depicting biblical characters, study them; they are a goldmine. Probably most of the windows refer to death in one way or another. Many memorialize persons now part of the church triumphant; probably there are adults in the parish whose history stretches back to days when these persons were alive. Some of them, given adequate time to prepare, might be happy to provide the leadership necessary for these explorations.

You may not be studying death directly, but God will be working deep within—as well as without—answering questions never asked in words that can be heard.

3. The *death of pets* is an experience with which almost every child is familiar, for almost everyone has grieved at the death of one of these friends. Ask the children to tell the story of the relationships they had with their pets. In their eyes and the tone of their voices you will hear love still close.[3]

4. *Visit a cemetery.* Many congregations maintain their own, or sections of larger ones. They are places where the church triumphant waits. Older parishioners may be willing to accompany you on your visit, and briefly reminisce here and there about friends and members now long dead.

5. *Visits to funeral homes* are helpful, not only for children but for adults. Toured as part of Sunday morning's church school, if possible, these places evoke many good questions. God cares for us all the while.

5. *Use the pall.* Instead of flowers, the pall is a large blanket used to cover each casket brought into the church. Like a warm quilt on a cold night, it symbolizes God's warm care for his children.

Often one sees in pictures and reportage that the first response of a loving parent or friend to a stricken child is to wrap the small body in a coat or other cloth.

Use the pall, bring it to your class, explore what it feels like to be covered and how it is to have a favorite blanket at night. In death

Death Lenten Topic
For Parish Children

By MELINDA FORBES
Beacon Staff Writer

EASTERN SHORE CHAPEL'S PARISH DAY SCHOOL:
CHILDREN LEARN THROUGH EXPLORING.

Beacon Photo by Melinda Forbes

Lent Program

Hanchey and Mrs. Garrison chat with preschoolers Lee Chafin (left), Doug Denny and Ashley Hanchey.

VIRGINIA BEACH — Although many people are buried in the cemetery at Eastern Shore Chapel, Jesus Christ Superstar is not among them.

When the students from the church's Parish Day School visited the graveyard and discussed who and what was buried there, one youngster pulled another aside and confidently told his buddy that Jesus Christ Superstar was buried in a nearby grave. It is while visiting the cemetary, holding picnics and nature hikes there and discussing the death of favorite pets, that these children are learning to come to terms with death and dying.

Lent, said the Rev. Howard Hanchey of the church, is a good time to discuss death and re-

birth, and each year he and the teachers at the school try to incorporate discussions about death and dying in their classrooms.

Death is something adults are reluctant to talk about with children, he said, but it is actually something very natural and the children accept it as long as they are not taught to fear it.

"We don't push it on them," he noted, "but if they want to talk about it and ask questions we are there to help answer them."

If a child brings in a dead bird, he said, "you can't deny it is dead." They need to be told something.

"It is adults who teach children to think death is something dreadful."

Actually, he said, death is as natural as birth, pain, or happiness and children see it as such until they find that adults fear it and they think they must fear it too.

By letting the pre-school students ask their questions about death, and by keeping the atmospthere light and natural instead of somber, the teachers hope to help the children continue to accept the idea of people dying.

Often, said Hanchey, the discussion will spring from the discovery of a dead insect or bird in the school yard, or by the death of a classmate's pet.

"Children are puzzled by death," said Mrs. Jean Rader "and are full of questions."

As soon as she takes her class back to the cemetery, she said, the children start talking about the graves and asking questions. Some of the comments like the one about superstar are priceless, she said.

They want to know about the gravestones, why the flowers are placed on the graves, how the dead are different from the living and why and what happened to them.

"We don't dwell on the subject," Mrs. Becky Garrison, a teacher in the school, said, "but we do take the time to answer any questions they have."

They know this is where the dead people are, Hanchey said, but to the children, the dead people are still part of the family   just resting in the cemetery.

Sometimes he said, the children want to know what it is like in the grave or what happened to the body.

At times he doesn't really have an answer to their questions, but feels the children are really more interested in having a way to explore death than they are in having an answer to every question.

To demonstrate the concept of death, Hanchey said he uses a candle. When it is lit it represents life and when the flame goes out it signifies dying.

He also plays a game with the children and answers questions such as can a dead person stand up, talk or move around.

He and the teachers have taken the children around the church and pointed out the stained glass windows in the sanctuary that show Christ on the cross and used that also to explain death.

"It is the children that are natural about death," Hanchey added, "and the adults who think death is unnatural. They have a lot to teach us."

before God, we are his alone, without any pretense as to our earthly achievements.

7. Some older members of the parish, if they know they are needed, might be willing to volunteer to *speak about death*, perhaps anticipating their own. Or they might be able to describe what it feels like to lose someone they loved.

The *Book of Common Prayer*, page 507, provides a touching reminder about human feelings in relation to death. It recalls Jesus weeping at the grave of his friend Lazarus (John 11:2f).[4]

8. *Plant some seeds* in a glass jar, right up next to the glass. Soon the children will see them sprout and realize that life can develop from something seemingly dead. St. Paul used a similar metaphor (1 Cor. 15:35–44), and it has been helpful to the Church ever since.

Discuss the seed's shriveled and wrinkled skin. Try to get into St. Paul's mind. What was he trying to teach, and use the seed imagery as a first-century person would.

9. Use the *seasons of the year*. By this time of the year, we are moving out of winter, and though on the surface it seems like a lifeless time, by relating the season's end to the seed planted, children can sense the close connection between life and death.

10. You may want to explore the *process of change*, how one thing dies and another is born, how the caterpillar becomes a moth or a butterfly and the tadpole becomes a frog. In many ways, to "find life," one must be prepared to "lose life" (Mt. 10:39).

These studies may not be for everyone, but good pastoral care and Christian education demand their inclusion in Sunday-school classes from time to time.

THE RISKING JESUS: SIX BIBLICAL STORIES

Jesus' life and ministry are another way to approach the impassioned side of our living. To care, Jesus was always risking himself in relationships. And so do we.

People thanked Jesus for what he brought. Sometimes, however, there were hostile, even punitive, replies. The following lessons highlight Jesus' activities evoking the "other side" of life.

You may choose to use these or other stories, but you won't be able to use them all. Remember, less is more. So enjoy, and make use of the chapter *Imaginative Bible Study*.

1. *Jesus and the Samaritan Woman (John 4: 1–42).* Whenever anyone wants to extend the hand of friendship to someone not generally accepted by his or her "group," there are always plenty of persons who protest loudly, ready with numerous reasons why such action is ill-advised. Christians need not "buy" this brand of self-righteousness—Jesus didn't; he accepted a cool drink of water from this "outcast" woman.

2. *The Pharisees Question a Man Cured (John 9:1–41).* A blind man is given sight, and others are outraged. The story has four scenes, each an interrogation. The degree of hostility increases from one scene to the next, and our lack of sympathy for other human beings is clearly illuminated by the light of Jesus' love and care. He put people first.

3. *Jesus Stops a Stoning (John 8:2–11).* Wads of paper for rocks have been used to "stone" a person caught in adultery, and someone playing the part of Jesus has entered to stop it.

Simple plays like this can be a powerful and interest-catching teaching device. Afterward, talk about what happened, wonder how it felt to be hurt, and how the woman felt when Jesus prevented her destruction.

4. *Overturning the Tables (Mark 11:15–19).* Everyone knows the story of Jesus' courage when he saw how people were mocking the temple. Jesus was a reformer, and the reformation theme might be given expression by a study of Martin Luther or John Wesley or John Calvin, among others. Some possibilities are noted in the next section.

5. *Jesus Gives Life to the Widow's Son (Luke 7:11–17).* These accounts too often sidetrack people into wondering if those involved were really dead or just in a coma. Approach them more simply, seeing in them still another instance in which Jesus' love evokes hostility and disbelief, but at the same time how they illuminate God's always-promised gift of life.

6. *Picking Corn on Sunday (Mark 2:23–28).* Jesus and his disciples provoke the Pharisees to protest his "law breaking." Jesus' response often has been cited by advocates of civil disobedience.

Once again the light shines, and we find ourselves required to examine the motives for our actions—and whether people come first, second, or last. What would you have done?

OTHERS WHO DARED: CHURCH HISTORY

Christian Church history shines with examples of people who loved God and risked their lives for him. They shaped their times, and marked human history with the stamp of their lives and vision. Some met with applause, but others risked both life and fortune. Like St. Stephen, they knew the gospel was true, and they pledged their lives to present it to the world.

Keep in mind that these suggestions are simply guides. You may use any or all. More suggestions are noted in the All-Saints section, and "store-bought" materials suggesting others abound. And don't forget your clergy: They are prepared to point you in the direction of other historical figures you may want to study.

1. *Robert Hunt.* Visitors to Jamestown, Virginia, can see a reconstructed village, the ruins of a brick church, and the old foundations of a number of buildings. There is also a bronze plaque with a picture of a communion service being held under a sail:

> To the Glory of God and in Memory of The Reverend Robert Hunt, Presbyter, appointed by the Church of England, Minister of the Colony which established the English Church and English civilization of Jamestown, Virginia, in 1607. . . . He planted the first Protestant church in America, and laid down his life in the foundations of Virginia.

Robert Hunt left a comfortable home in England to sail with one hundred sixty men in three tiny, crowded ships to the New World. He was their minister. On May 14, 1607, the ships landed at the mouth of the James River, in Jamestown. As the men came ashore, Robert Hunt offered prayers of thanksgiving to God, and the first English settlement in America was begun.

There was much to be done that first week. The ships had to be unloaded, a fort and small houses begun, gardens planted, food hunted in the forest and fished from the sea. The ships also had to be loaded with lumber and made ready for the long, dangerous journey back to England.

But when Sunday came the men stopped to worship. They hung a sailcloth between the trees, made an altar from a plank, and set lengths of tree trunks for their pews. This was their church, and under that sailcloth the Reverend Robert Hunt conducted the first communion service, June 21, 1607. The Church of God took root in America.

2. *Joan of Arc.* Joan was condemned as a heretic in 1431 and, at age nineteen, burned at the stake by the English. She was made a saint in 1920. Her life and ministry illustrate the conflict between good and evil, and how these forces are sometimes intertwined.

Joan was caught between the hypocrisies of the Church and the politics of the state. She was a French patriot who fought the English when they occupied France. She organized armies, led the French in battle, and crowned a king whose family had been removed from the throne. She was subsequently betrayed, persecuted, and burned at the stake, convicted by a French Church court and delivered to the English for execution.

She struggled with disappointment and grief as she was condemned to death.

3. *John Wycliffe (1320–1384).* Just as the monk Jerome translated the Bible from Greek and Hebrew into Latin so that God's message might be read by many, so an Englishman, John Wycliffe, translated the Latin Vulgate into English for the same reason.

Christian Church authorities and leaders in government feared people might become unruly if they read the Bible for themselves, so they did all they could to destroy the copies Wycliffe made. But as copies were found and destroyed, more copies were made, even though each had to be written by hand and in secrecy.

Those who read the Bible, or even listened to it being read, were punished. Some were burned at the stake.

Wycliffe died a natural death before he could be caught and punished, but forty-four years after his death, Church authorities had his body exhumed and burned and the ashes tossed into a nearby stream.

4. *William Tyndale (1494–1536).* Tyndale was a devout and determined man. He was aware that only a Bible written in the English language of his own day could satisfy his people's hunger for the Scriptures. He knew most people were poor and many could not afford John Wycliffe's handwritten copies. He also knew the Church punished those who tried to make the Bible available to everyone. To one such authority he said,

> If God spare my life, ere many years I will cause a boy that driveth
> a plough to know more of the Scripture than thou doest.

So Tyndale set about his task of making a new translation. The year Tyndale had finished college, Erasmus's Greek New Testament had been published. He compared this source with the Latin Vulgate as the basis of his translation of the New Testament. His Old Testament was drawn from the Hebrew texts.

Tyndale was later arrested and put to death. "Lord, open thou the King of England's eyes" were his prayerful words as he was burned at the stake.

5. St. Stephen.   St. Stephen was the first of the early Christians killed because of his response to the gospel. The story of his life has already been discussed here.

6. Robert Raikes.   A statue of Robert Raikes stands near London's River Thames. Mr. Raikes is described there as the founder of Sunday schools.

Robert Raikes had the good luck to inherit a fortune and a newspaper while he was still a young man. Anyone who owned a newspaper was aware of what was going on in town, and Mr. Faikes discovered all was not right in Gloucester.

In those days (circa 1780) children were hired to work in mills and factories; they had no chance to go to school as ours do. On Sundays, their only day of rest, there was nothing for them to do but roam the streets and get into trouble. Robert Raikes decided to do something about it, and so he started a Sunday school.

Not everyone was happy about it. The mill and factory owners did not want the children educated, for then the latter might realize they were being overworked and underpaid. A few Church authorities objected to *anyone* working on Sunday, even if it were to teach. Nonetheless, Raikes went ahead.

The teachers were women. They were paid one shilling and sixpence to teach reading and Bible lessons. The Sunday school was held on a street called Sooty Alley.

The first good effect the new school had on the city of Gloucester was the quiet that was observed on Sundays while the children were in school instead of "raising hell" (as one editorial put it) in the streets. Within six years there were two hundred thousand children in England going to Sunday school.

GOD'S GOOD FRIDAY—TODAY: A STUDY FOR LENT

Why is there suffering in the world? Jeremiah (Jer. 12:1) puts it another way: Why do the ways of the wicked prosper?

In this section I want to pay close attention to always troublesome questions about pain, suffering and abuse in the world, questions often asked by older teens and adults.

Natural faith—a faith generated by God's presence in our lives— is easily begun by God, and we explored its birth and growth in chapter 4. The older we grow the more we are confronted by the harsh realities of life, and from adolescence onward natural faith takes the shape of a search for more comprehensive understandings. When these explorations take place in the Christian community of faith, natural faith can begin to become Christian, and Christian faith deepens, because God's given the opportunity to provide some answers to our questions.[5]

Lent is a grand time for these studies.[6]

1. *Life and Death in Marty's Life.*   Marty writes this:

I recently experienced what I've come to believe is God's presence at the burial of a young man. He had been an active member of my parish.

The days preceding the graveside service were particularly emotional. He was the victim of a drunk driver, he was 16 years of age, and he was an honor student and an acolyte captain.

The young people of the parish, one of whom included one of my daughters, were particularly distraught.

After the shocking news, several hectic days and a crowded church service, my daughter and I went to a small graveside service in Arlington Cemetery. There were only his family and a few friends.

As our worship ended, my daughter turned to speak to me. I motioned to her to be still, thinking that family and friends might like to bid a silent prayer before leaving.

But a silence began to grow. We all seemed to be brought together, and a sense of gentle, quiet peace began to engulf us.

I found myself breathing a sigh of relief from the previous days of tension, allowing a feeling of weightlessness to enfold me.

And then it dawned on me: I knew God was there. It was like a moment of resurrection. It was God who was in the silent, restful stillness.

Or maybe better, it was God who was the silent and restful stillness.

It is a mystery to me yet. But what God's presence brought was peace, humility and praise for having known this young man—one who'd been in my home many times.

How does this happen? I really don't know. Only that it does, though I wish for it more than just occasionally.

Marty is a Christian, and her ability to identify God's presence in the midst of life is a characteristic of Christian faith.

She has come to expect peaceful moments like that described above. Also, she knows who it is who stands in the shadows, keeping watch over his own. [7]

2. *The Bible Illuminates.* Scripture helps us identify signs of God's presence and ministry in the here and now of everyday life, just as a flashlight helps us see a path in the dark, and several Bible passages illuminate Marty's experience.

"God is our refuge and strength, a very present help in trouble. Therefore we will not fear . . ."

[Psalm 46:1]

And at another time,

". . . And behold, the Lord passed by, and a great and strong wind rent the mountains, and broke in pieces the rocks before the Lord, but the Lord was not in the wind; and after the wind an earthquake, but the Lord was not in the earthquake; and after the earthquake a fire, but the Lord was not in the fire; and after the fire a still small voice."

[I Kings 19:11ff]

God is present in our lives. It is not hard to anticipate his consoling response to a grieving community. At the funeral God did what he always does best—he was present, helping a community support its members and bringing the possibility of communion to a people fractured by loss.

3. *The Power of God.* Like Marty (and many of us), I too have felt the presence of God as power. At such times I have felt the presence of another who appears all through the pages of the Bible, not that God is ever absent in the midst of life, but sometimes we are more aware of his presence than at other times.

Because of God's presence a sense of *shalom,* or peacefulness, took shape around Marty. This is not the peace of Rome, the *pax romana,* a peace imposed from the outside, but a wholesome sense of quietude.

Similar feelings emerge also in liturgical worship, especially at festivals when the whole community of faith is especially expectant. These feelings of wholeness often take a powerful shape, even to the point of causing tears.

4. Using Bible-Imaginative Speculation. Still the question remains: Why didn't God prevent this senseless death?

Bible-imaginative speculation, presented in Chapter 4, is particularly helpful with hard questions like these.

Bible-imaginative speculation requires that we work with a story from everyday life (like Marty's) and ask two questions:

1. What is God's ministry in this event, and
2. What signs can I see of his presence?

Bible-imaginative speculation never begins from the point of view of ideas alone, it always begins with a story taken from the here and now of everyday life. Particularly when working with teens, always begin with a story from their lives or one about which they are excited.

5. Human Freedom: To Create and To Destroy. The fact is, long before God began healing a community injured by loss, God was passing judgment on one having too much to drink. Surely God cautioned against "one more drink," and surely he judged wrong the decision "I'll drive home." God is not silent, and God cares.

The word "conversation" is rooted in the Latin *con* and *versari*, meaning to travel with. The Bible is a long book about God's journey with the people of Israel and the early church. God was not silent then and God is not silent now. God cares, and although it may look like God is not very interested in events like these, Scripture says otherwise, and eyes of faith see more.

God made us in his image, and just as he is free to create and destroy, so are we. We are not robots simply marching to his orders.

Like Adam and Eve in the garden, we too can choose our own way. This does not mean, however, that God is uninterested or absent, and most of all it does not mean he is silent. It *does* mean that God, for the sake of our freedom to create the way he creates, set us free to destroy as he never does (and wishes that we didn't).

Just as this drunk driver was free to decide to drive and risk destruction, so too we are free—all the time. Add to our destructive capacity the survival of the fittest—wanting things our way, at the expense of all else—and you have the reason for the destruction in the world. POINT. Our God-given freedom to create brings with it the freedom to destroy. Destruction in the world is a consequence of human freedom, and before we blame God for it, we do far better to look closely at our own responsibility, or lack of it.

If it weren't for our freedom, there would be no human imagination, no curiosity, and no capacity to dream. Everything would be fixed and permanently in place, and we would be robots not made in the image of God.

Life may not be fair, and often neither are we to one another. But God is fair and closely present, working hard to bring order out of the chaos we too often make. He suffers with us (Heb. 2:9), and though we struggle in our suffering, we are not alone in it (2 Cor. 1:1–8), for God is there with us (Phil. 3:10).

6. *Why Bad Things Happen.* God, having limited himself, becoming powerless in relation to our freedom of choice, cannot weave the tapestry of our lives—nor world history—as quickly as he might like.

Hence, human patience is not a virtue because it *ought* to be a virtue; it is the shape of God's ministry, which, given the constraints he has placed on his power, means that it often takes him great lengths of time, given the many variables of our lives, to work things out. It took God forty years and a lot of patience to get the Hebrews through the wilderness. It could have been done sooner if God had simply forced their march, but that would have violated their freedom and made them less than human. And ultimately it would have coerced their love—making it no love at all.

Jesus could have used his power to show his strength by giving in to the temptations at the beginning of his ministry, but this is not God's way. Self-initiated love is that for which he longs.

God would no more abuse a driver considering another drink than reject his world, though this doesn't at all mean he was silent, nor his judgment not perfectly clear in the moment. Still, we are free (aren't we?) to listen . . . or not (at least in the life of this world).

So what is God to do? Just this: God helps us take care of a world he calls his own. Now there are Mothers Against Drunk Driving (MADD) and Students Against Drunk Driving (SADD), and the list goes on and on. Though we may continue to use alcohol to excess, as community consciousness increases, it becomes increasingly difficult for responsible people to act carelessly. To eyes of faith, these are clear signs of God's ministry.

Much of God's ministry in the world is spent picking up the pieces of what we do to one another, and though God may be powerless in the moment, God is never impotent long-term.

7. *The Powerlessness of God.* I worked for several years as a full-time chaplain in a hospital, and there, with others, I was engaged by God's powerlessness.

I readily confess I've experienced my own powerlessness in the helping relationship. I have felt it most acutely at the bedside of those patients alive to a pain there is no narcotic to ease. I still feel powerless with couples raging at one another, negotiating for divorce and threatening one another for the custody of children. I have learned to expect to be powerless in the helping relationship. Indeed, I *am* powerless.

It is precisely here that I have also felt the presence of God as powerless. Not hopeless, but a sense in which if God could have it otherwise, what the "other" is experiencing would be put aside.

This is not mere projection of my powerlessness on to God, but God's presence as powerless, closely connected with deep loving care and grief.

I have felt God's powerlessness when a couple, raging at one another, glimpse, for a brief moment, what once was and cannot be again, and crash on toward the destruction of a relationship which began with such hope. In such places as these God's grieving presence is felt.

8. *Making Things New.* So what does God do? God is always about the business of making things new.

The Bible shows God creating newness three ways. God 1. creates from nothing, 2. raises the dead to life, and 3. transforms the living.[8]

Now God is free to raise from the dead, and does so when asked by Elijah (I Kings 17) and Jesus (John 11:28–44). And God is just as free to create from nothing, and here is the story of creation (from Genesis), and the story as well of the formation of MADD and SADD. At the funeral, God also from nothing began to generate a sense of shalom, though doubtless he was also responding to the prayers of those who were asking for solace.

At none of these times was there any imposition of God's will on creation. God was either making things new from nothing, or reviving the shattered hearts of friends and family.

But God can only make us new if we respond. God will not "do a number" on us. Force is not of God, and St. Paul is a preeminent example (Acts 9:3–9), not to mention your lives and mine.[9]

If God is one who stands at the door of our lives and knocks, we are the ones to open (Rev. 3:20). Here was, I suspect, the shape of God's ministry and his powerlessness as one of his own considered the possibility of—and decided to take—one more drink. God spoke, and God was ignored.

9. *Human Freedom and God's Faithfulness.* We are free, in every case, to turn from God and not acknowledge his hoped-for communion with us. We are free to turn toward our own ends alone. The Bible begins with this note.

Still, God keeps company with us. His is a company kept for better and for worse, for richer for poorer, in sickness and in health. His is company that not only rejoices with us but suffers with us.

The question of God's power and powerlessness is complex, but its consideration highlights the freedom God has given us and details human responsibility as no other focus can.

10. *Planning Classroom Activity.* By way of classroom plans, take Bible stories about bad things, stories from the daily newspaper or stories from the experience of the members of your class (if class members aren't embarrassed), and reflect on them from the perspectives suggested in this section.

Pay careful attention to signs of newness. How do these signs match up with the picture of God painted in the Bible? Where are there signs of God's powerlessness, and what might he have counseled in the moment as a destructive action developed?

Bible-imaginative speculation affords a splendid opportunity to understand the shape of God's ministry in our midst, the strength of human freedom and his grief in the story being considered.

The Action/Reflection approach to storytelling—detailed in Chapter 5—is particularly helpful, and the discussion of faith's development in the same chapter tells us what to expect.

Encourage a search, and God will write the truth of the matter in the moment of your discussion.

FLOWERING A CROSS AND MAKING AN EASTER-EGG TREE

Easter is the preeminent celebration of Jesus' resurrection. Every Sunday may be called a "little Easter," but the one in spring is the major festival of the Church year. For us teachers the question is: How can we help children celebrate it?

A cross can be flowered, and its "dead" wood, dressed with flowers and greenery, shines with life, light, and color. It is a vivid symbol of the resurrection.

In southern climates, garden flowers may be readily available. Not so in the north. In cool, springlike climates, potted plants (in 2" and 3" pots) can be bulk purchased from a local nursery. Instead of pinning them to a wooden cross, the cross can be constructed with small boxes to hold the pots. Even if the cross is tilted there is little danger of the pots falling out, and the potted plants later can be set in the ground around the church or at home. Throughout the summer, as they grow they remind us of Easter, again and again.

An Easter-Egg Tree is also an appropriate expression of the day's celebration. The egg and the butterfly are two of the earliest symbols of the resurrection; both represent life and transformation.

The eggs can be prepared during the latter weeks of Lent and, at home or in the Sunday classroom, brightly colored and hung on a bare branch on Easter Sunday. The bare branch might be likened to one growing out of the stump of Jesse (Isaiah 11:1–2)—a forebear of Jesus—or a branch adorned with the glory of God, like that described in Isaiah 4:2.

If Easter Sunday does not allow for the inclusion of the tree or flowered cross, it can be saved until the first Sunday of Easter, sometimes characterized as Low Sunday.

All this is fun, isn't it? The following are some Sunday-classroom activities.

FIRST SUNDAY:

—Which teaching focus will you use?
—What is passionate activity in the lives of your pupils?
—How do people hurt one another?
—How does hurting one another affect the quality of community life?
—We need a bulletin-board presentation on the theme of Lent.
—Consider how you might talk about death.
—There can be an instructed Burial Office.
—Plant a seed or bulb now for "resurrection."

SECOND SUNDAY:

—How do people "fast" today?
—Study Jesus helping others.

—Study Jesus' angry response to injustice in his day.
—Look closely at some of the suggested persons from Church history.
—Are you exploring Stephen's love for the Lord?
—What were the consequences for him?
—Can you develop a play about Stephen?
—Is the Christian-education bulletin board up to date?

THIRD SUNDAY:

—The instructed Burial Office may be offered today.
—Explore the Burial Office.
—Why do we use a pall?
—Why do we sing great hymns at the burial of the dead?
—Have you ever wondered what death is like? (Your pupils probably have.)
—How is your "dead" seed growing?
—Use First Corinthians 15:35–43. St. Paul says, "What you sow does not come to life unless it dies" and "What is sown is perishable and what is raised is imperishable" and "It is sown a physical body and it is raised a spiritual body."
—Don't forget the images of the mustard seed in Matthew 13:31, Mark 4:31, and Luke 13:19.
—Plant some flower seeds now in flats so they can be transplanted in the spring to places around the church—on Rogation Sunday.
—What is it like to dare to care, to take a chance for other people?
—Look over the Passion Gospel for Palm Sunday.
—Wonder how Jesus felt.
—Remind your students about the great Easter liturgy.
—What are other teachers doing?

FOURTH SUNDAY:

—How is your bulb growing?
—Examine it—the roots, the part reaching for the surface.
—Make an Easter basket of grass seeds for the very young.
—Have you thought of inviting parents to class to discuss a lesson?
—How about the Easter/Pentecost bulletin board?
—How about a trip to the cemetery?
—Where are the buried persons who were members of our

church? Now a part of the church triumphant—they are still
a part of us.
—Let your children wonder how that is.
—How about scheduling a trip to a funeral home?
—Can the clergy of the parish help?
—Will there be enough garden flowers to flower the cross on
Easter?
—Remind your class of Palm Sunday's Passion Gospel reading.
—Don't forget the Maundy Thursday stripping and washing of
the altar.

FIFTH SUNDAY:

—How is your garden growing?
—Have any of your pupils' pets ever died?
—Listen to the children tell their stories.
—Look at the pall. (Ask the Altar Guild to show it to you.)
—Wonder with your class how St. Stephen felt as he was stoned.
—Remind your class about Palm Sunday and Maundy Thursday.

SIXTH SUNDAY:

—Palm Sunday.
—In this liturgy palms will be given out—there will be a great
procession—and the Passion Gospel will be dramatically read.
—Wonder what Pontius Pilate felt like.
—Wonder how Jesus felt.
—What happened to Jesus next?
—Encourage your children to come to church on Maundy Thurs-
day night.

MAUNDY THURSDAY:

—The stripping and washing of the altar.
—In this evening service the altar is stripped, the candles put
out, and everything is darkened. It follows on Palm Sunday
worship and fuses together the experience of death with the
Easter resurrection.
—It is powerful worship.

GOOD FRIDAY:

—The time of the cross.

EASTER EVE:

—A time for baptisms and the Liturgy of Light.

EASTER SUNDAY:
—The Festival Eucharist of the Resurrection.
—A parish party follows.

Notes

1. *The Hymnal of the Protestant Episcopal Church, 1940* (New York: The Church Pension Fund, 1940), Hymn 62.
2. Ibid., Hymn 71.
3. Melinda Forbes, "Death Lenten Topic for Parish Children," *The Virginia Beach Beacon,* 7 April 1976. Published as part of *The Ledger-Star* and *The Virginian-Pilot,* Norfolk, VA.
4. Wayne E. Oates, *Pastoral Care and Counseling in Grief and Separation* (Philadelphia: Fortress Press, 1976). Oates poses the helpful notion of "death education" in the overall spiritual instruction of a congregation (page 19). He has a point, and Lent is an opportune time to explore such topics as death, funerals, ministry to the sick and the bereaved, and those suffering loss either by death, separation, or divorce. Such a range of topics need not be approached every year, but it should be handled with some regularity in the life of the parish.
5. Biblical stories entail numerous possibilities for a discussion of God's power and powerlessness. Calvary was an event without peer, and so was the slaughter of the innocents, as were almost all of the events recounted during the Lenten term. The ways and means to explore these stories, from this perspective, are discussed in the chapter *Imaginative Bible Study,* the sections *How To Tell Great Stories—VI* and *Storytelling for Young Children, Teens, and Adults.*
6. Thomas C. Oden, *Pastoral Theology: Essentials in Ministry* (Cambridge: Harper and Row, 1983), 223–48. A brief and thoughtful discussion, from the perspective of pastoral care, of the relationships among God's power, God's powerlessness (or self-limitation), and human freedom.
See also: Dietrich Bonhoeffer, *Prisoner for God: Letters and Papers from Prison,* trans. Reginald H. Fuller (New York: The Macmillan Co., 1954); "God Without Religion," April 30, 1944, pp. 121–24; "The Powerlessness of God," July 9, 1944, pp. 161–64; "Repentance," July 21, 1944, pp. 168–69. Bonhoeffer, in the midst of Hitler's terrible exercise of power, struggled to make sense of God's provi-

dence, human freedom, and the holocaust then taking place. Bonhoeffer was hanged by the Gestapo in 1944.

Some biblical allusions to the powerlessness of God: Mt. 19:20–22; Mk. 3:29, 10:20–22, 35–45; Lk. 18:21–23; Phil. 2:6–11.

Some biblical allusions to the power of God denied: Mt. 4:1–11, 26:51–55.

7. *The Hymnal of the Protestant Episcopal Church, 1940,* Hymn 519.

8. Walter Brueggemann, "Covenanting as Human Vocation," *Interpretation, A Journal of Bible and Theology* 33, no. 2 (April 1979): 118. Brueggemann's summary of God's creative capacity is the foundation for my discussion of God's power and its opposite, God's powerlessness. Further, his article (though perhaps too demanding for those unfamiliar with theology) is nevertheless very helpful in the formulation of a theology for Sunday-morning Christian education.

9. *The Hymnal of the Protestant Episcopal Church, 1940,* Hymn 298.

CHAPTER THIRTEEN

The Easter/Pentecost Term: Made for Life

The Easter/Pentecost term is an eight-week celebration of Easter. God's promise of new life is its major theme. Depending on when Easter falls, this term can be long or short, so develop your educational plans accordingly.

Just as in every other term, there is more material here than any one class can handle in a year. So set some limits, and expect to have fun with fewer topics.

WINDING DOWN AND SAYING GOODBYE

Several comments about this term's atmosphere are in order. There are two elements over which we have little control.

A "Low Sunday" syndrome seems to characterize this term.

"Low Sunday" is the name some Christians traditionally call the Sunday following Easter Day. Show me a church whose attendance is not below the previous Easter Day, and I will show you the Kingdom of God . . . coming fast. Having anticipated Easter so eagerly and celebrated it so fully, it is almost as if we need to back off a bit, emotionally.

The more intensive explorations of Epiphany and Lent will not take place this term, and good education does not force a process for which there is no longer energy or enthusiasm.

THE FACT IS: The year is just about finished, and everyone knows it. Public-school sessions are winding down, spring is in the air, summer vacations are near, and classrooms are too tight for expansive souls. It is unrealistic to expect the intensity and focused concentration of midyear teaching and learning; the cross-current of separation is simply too great.

As teachers, we do ourselves a real disservice by not taking account of endings. If we expect the same intensity and enthusiasm that characterized the other terms, we run the risk of disappointment—and our students will suffer as well.

I wish things were not this way. I would prefer to see the lively enthusiasm of the fall persist, particularly in the spring. But our culture—what with the end of the public-school year, summer vacations, and all the rest—just does not make this kind of spirited atmosphere possible.

Nevertheless, there is some excitement left, even if it is not quite what we might like it to be. Instead of fighting a battle to enliven the flagging student interest, use what remains, and have fun with it.

If you find something you would really like to explore this term but cannot, remember that the All-Saints term in the fall continues this term's theme; maybe you can teach it then. The seasonal terms facilitate this kind of follow-up.

PREREGISTRATION FOR THE FALL

If the year has gone well and enthusiasm has been generated all along, you will have little trouble finding out who is going to attend Sunday school next year. Granted, some people may have already taken off for the summer, and attendance may be down; that is to be expected. But most folks are still around, and a parishwide registration push will get you in good shape for the fall.

This term's worship will also help. The blessing of the animals is a joyful event, and with the Ascension and Pentecost celebrations ending the term—along with a grandly ceremonious graduation day—everything will work together to draw lots of pupils for next year.

Preregistration is not, however, the task of the teaching personnel; it is the task of clergy and the Sunday-school superintendent. Or better, a task for the Christian-education committee of the Board or Vestry. So look sharp, and get going on next year.

THE WAYS AND MEANS OF TEACHING

There is no way all the suggested topics can be used this term, so note those that especially interest you.

An enthusiastic teacher is in the ideal position to lead the class. Be prepared to set limits on subject matter and to develop lesson plans with yourself in mind.

POINT: Absences this term will begin to increase, so build your curriculum so that each Sunday's work can stand by itself.

Some classes may decide to fashion a banner depicting the events they intend to study. Or they may choose to create a chancel drama for themselves, for other classes, or for presentation in Sunday morning's main worship.

Learning is thereby facilitated, and whatever emerges can also be used on graduation Sunday. The whole parish benefits.

Consider, too, devoting your class to the task of designing the Christian-education bulletin board. The board will be up for most of the summer. It often acts as a great beacon, attracting parishioners to teach next year's classes.

What is the best of all reasons for this kind of activity? Simply:

I hear and I forget.

I see and I remember.

I do and I understand.

ST. PAUL: FOUR TOPICS FOR CLASSROOM STUDY

Paul is, in some sense, every one of us, so his experience and pilgrimage are not confined to the first century. From when he knew very little of Jesus, to a time of intense antagonism toward the early Church, to a still later encounter, conversion, and growth in the early Christian community of faith, Paul's life touches the major currents that shape the hearts and minds of Christians.

St. Paul was one of the last persons to meet the risen Christ (Acts 9f). On a trip to Damascus, intending to expand his persecutions of the early Church, Paul's attitude and life were radically transformed. He heard the words, "Saul, Saul, why do you persecute me?" In that moment Paul became a new creation—no longer persecutor but witness. The period of Paul's growth as a Christian was, however, considerably longer than those few minutes; it lasted a couple of years.

In every generation since, Christians have walked a path like Paul's. The particulars may be different, but the movement is the same. First, there is always a sense of not knowing, then an awareness that touches our senses, and then the journey begins. Once on it, we, like Paul, listen closely to stories about Jesus, the works he did and the parables he used.

1. *Stories of the Resurrection.* Paul's immediate reaction was to retreat, first to regain his sight, then to reflect deeply on what had happened. Later he began to involve himself in the early Church. He heard the stories of Jesus' ministry, probably meeting face to face with persons like Thomas, Mary, Peter, and Cleopas, all of whom had seen Jesus after the resurrection.

Along with the rest of the early Church gathered in small groups near the city of Jerusalem, Paul would have heard of *Cleopas* and his friend who, traveling to the village *Emmaus,* were joined by a third person. On that journey of seven or so miles, impressed with their visitor's knowledge of Scripture, they invited him to break bread with them at the day's-end meal. As their visitor took the bread, gave thanks, broke it, and gave it to them, they suddenly recognized their new friend to be the Lord himself (Luke 24:13–34). Now terribly excited, and because the visitor had left, they rushed straight back to Jerusalem, only to discover he had been there, too.

Paul probably also met *Thomas,* listening to him recall with vivid imagery the experience of touching the wounds on Jesus' body (John 20:24f).

He might have heard how Jesus joined some of his friends and *ate fish* one evening (Luke 24:41f), and he would certainly have heard, perhaps firsthand, how *Mary Magdalene, Joanna,* and *Mary the mother of James* had seen the empty tomb (Luke 24:10f).

A hungry Paul would have eagerly gobbled up every one of these stories. The imagery was vivid and the excitement contagious.

These and other recollections of other appearances are found at the end of each of the four Gospels. Here are some suggestions for teaching these stories.

Pretend you are St. Paul, hearing these stories for the first time. What would you have thought? What would you have felt? And remember, you are hearing stories about a man, crucified, dead, and buried, who had met you on the road to Damascus.

Your class might also be interested in comparing the accounts in Matthew, Mark, and Luke. Choose one Gospel, and use the ends of the others as a field for a treasure hunt, looking for the similar story.

The language sometimes varies, mainly because in the early days of the Church few of these stories were written down and each person heard them a little bit differently than the others. By the time the stories were written, maybe thirty years after the resurrection, and because of the deaths of the first eyewitnesses, many had been retold variously, reflecting the unique memories of the tellers.

Another teacher may want to help his or her class make pictures of the events or explore the feelings of the participants as they confronted the mystery of their friend and teacher raised to life. Alive again!

Still others may want to reconstruct the journey of Cleopas and his friend as they were joined by the other.

Jesus almost always appeared in the context of a meal, as those who knew him ate together and reminisced.

Early Christians learned that Eucharist is the way the Last Supper continues, so every time they worshiped they looked for Jesus to be present. We do, too. And still, he is.

2. Stories of Jesus Bringing Life.   In those first days of the Church (and grand days they were), besides accounts of the resurrection, early Christians inevitably recalled stories of Jesus' ministry.

Along with others, Paul would have heard of the blind *Bartimaeus* (Mark 10:46f), how Jesus healed *ten lepers* (Luke 17:11f) and only one returned to thank him.

Paul would have heard the story of when a *Roman Centurion* appealed to Jesus to heal a sick servant whom he loved (Luke 7:1f). Paul would have been keenly touched by Jesus' response.

All these stories are found in the four Gospels. Some appear several times. For the most part, they are arranged in chronological order. The clear point through them all, however, is the witness that Jesus is special and that in his life the full power of God's love was always immediately present and available.

This theme for study is found in the chapter *Imaginative Bible Study* and the Epiphany section, *Telling the Good News Stories of Jesus.*

3. Parables Jesus Used to Explain Life.   In addition to stories of the resurrection and recollections of healings, Jesus' parables would have teased St. Paul's interest.

Like other Christians in the first century, Paul was probably familiar with Jesus' story of a *Samaritan* who, on a trip, gave aid to a man who had been beaten by robbers (Luke 10:29f).

I suspect he also heard the story of a *prodigal son* and a father's forgiveness (Luke 15:11f), surely a lesson not lost on him. He probably also heard about a poor man named *Lazarus*, who starved outside the gate of a rich man (Luke 16:19f).

In each of these stories, Paul undoubtedly heard a message of God's love and care as Jesus used rich illustrations to describe the kingdom of heaven.

When approaching these studies, try to get into Paul's skin as a new-born Christian. What did he hear in Jesus' parables? By doing so, God will write the truth of the matter in the hearts of your young pupils.

Stories of Jesus' giving care and the parables he told lend themselves to dramatic presentation. Don't miss the potential for learning inherent in short plays. *Godspell* is compelling evidence of drama's communicative powers.

The chapter titled *Imaginative Bible Study* also provides a number of useful tools.

4. *Paul Helps God Build the Church.* Some of you may choose to study Paul during the All-Saints term. If you studied St. Stephen's martyrdom during Lent, Paul would be found there, too (Acts 8). None of the other terms, however, provides for the extensive exploration of Paul's conversion and ministry as does this one. Paul's response to the risen Christ led to the formation of small Christian congregations throughout Asia Minor and as far away as eastern Europe and Rome. People heard good news in Paul's voice. They heard it in the words he chose and in the stories he told.

Though there was no one in the bleachers recording how he went about it, he must have presented the gospel well, for people heard the good news in Galatia, Philippi, Ephesus, and Corinth.

His method might have looked like this:

a. He might have said with enthusiasm, "I've got some good news."

b. "Let me tell you of a fellow named John, called the Baptist. He baptized a lot of people in a river called Jordan. But that's not the point, really; rather, he was preparing for the life and ministry of a man named Jesus."

c. Paul would have then described Jesus' ministry, his enthusiasm mounting.

d. He might have continued by commenting that it is not so much

Jesus' ministry that is important but that he "met me *after* he was dead. In fact, he is alive."

e. Then Paul would have concluded more personally, "It has affected me this way . . . ," followed by an elaboration on his enthusiasm for the Gospel's certain promise of life for God's world.

There would have been little talk of Palestine in the Pauline Gospel. The people of Asia Minor had no maps, and the names of cities and geographic regions would have been of little interest to them.

POINT: Those who heard, *if* they believed, believed because of the things Paul said about Jesus. They were touched by Paul's enthusiasm and God's spirited interest.

Out of events like these arose a Church. Some in the crowd caught a vision of their God's sovereign power and love, one whom Jesus called, in Hebrew, *abba,* or father.

Before Paul left, persons might well have asked, "Would you say that again?" or "Tell me that in a little different way; maybe I can catch it this time." Thus, small communities of Christians were formed.

Matthew, Mark, and Luke get most of the credit for recording these stories about Jesus. And that is sad, for Paul had been preaching the good news of God's promise of life at least ten years before it was put to paper by these three, and his earliest epistle predates Mark's Gospel by several years.

Because most Christians recall Paul's stern admonitions to the small, new churches spread throughout Asia Minor, he is remembered, primarily, as a man of judgment. It is tragic, for Paul did not establish the Church by preaching judgment. That is the last thing to bring people together.

In a way, Paul was caught in an administrative trap. New churches, like families, lived together not only for better but for worse. So Paul, sometimes several months' journey distant, used the written word to respond to the issues arising in their common life. Every one of these small churches looked to him for guidance, and because they were so few, word of their struggles had a way of reaching Paul.

When the church at Corinth began to abuse the Lord's table, it was Paul who wrote (I Cor. 11:17f) to its leaders, encouraging a more compassionate response to one another.

When words of clarification about an issue were called for, it was Paul to whom the young churches looked.

Through Paul a nurturing God brought order to small Church

families struggling to "keep the faith." Though we do not have a copy
of the Gospel according to St. Paul, it might read a lot like St. Mark's,
the earliest written.

You can explore with your classes the kinds of questions those who
heard Paul's Gospel might have asked. What stimulated the listeners'
curiosity? What feelings were generated as stories were told of Jesus
bringing sight to the blind?

Other studies suggested by Paul's life and ministry might center
on his missionary journeys: Just where did he go, and with whom?

STORIES OF THE GOOD SHEPHERD

The Fourth Sunday of Easter, for Episcopalians, has always been
designated Good Shepherd Sunday, not officially but affectionately—
just as the third Sunday of Advent, for Episcopalians, is known as
"Stir-Up" Sunday, because of its collect. The Collect for the Day and
the lessons designated by the lectionary, for Episcopalians and most
Christians, elaborate on the Good Shepherd motif. Several weeks'
lessons can be built around this theme.

MAKING USE OF PARISH WORSHIP

Worship continues to be a major part of Sunday-school education;
even as class enthusiasm wanes, it continues to generate enthusiasm.
Consider the following five opportunities.

A BLESSING OF THE ANIMALS

The middle of May is a first-rate time to think about blessing some
animals. St. Francis would like it, and so would the authors of Genesis. They charge us to be carefully responsible for all God's creatures.[1,2]

The liturgy itself makes use of hymns like "All Things Bright and
Beautiful," "Fairest Lord Jesus," "Shining Day," and "Now Thank We
All Our God."[3] Flor Peeters' "March of the Animals" is a bright piece,
and "A Song of Creation" (page 88, *The Book of Common Prayer*)
picks up the afternoon's theme.

The prayer for the animals—recited when the recipients are presented—reads: "May God so bless this pet of yours, that your love for it may be a reflection of God's love for you."

THE MORNING RECORD
—and Journal
6— Meriden, Ct.,   Tuesday, May 31, 1977

God's creatures blessed at St. Andrew's service

"All the animals were sitting there, just looking around the church, as though they had been doing it all their lives," Margaret Turner, Meriden Humane Society president, said.

"I sat in the back of the church and watched all the big dogs sitting quietly. It was a very wonderful feeling," she said, describing the "Service for the Blessing of God's Animals," at St. Andrew's Episcopal Church, Sunday afternoon.

The Rev. Dr. Howard Hanchey, rector of St. Andrew's, celebrated the relationship between a child and his or her pet in a Memorial weekend worship service unique to this area. Approximately 70 animals — cats, kittens, toads, dogs, birds and goldfish — accompanied by their people, sat attentively throughout the service and patiently waited to be individually blessed.

While organist Stephen Tappe performed Flor Peter's "March of the Animals," pets and persons assembled in the church to hear the creation story from Genesis and sing several hymns about animals specially selected for the occasion. Prayers were offered for hungry, lost and homeless animals.

Children and other pet owners listened as Dr. Hanchey urged them to take responsibility for their animals, just as God takes responsibility for His people. The rector stressed the special relationship which exists between a child and animal

friends. The service was created by Dr. Hanchey, who has participated in similar celebrations at his former parish in Virginia.

The procession of animals to the front of the church for the blessing was spontaneous and not marred by any of the chaos which might be expected from a church full of 70 mixed animals.

"There were numerous types of dogs, a cat with seven kittens, and one young boy with a jar of fish," Miss Turner said.

"I was a little skeptical at first. I thought some of the dogs might get out of control. But they were beautiful. None of the dogs were snippy or mean. They actually seemed to enjoy it."

A relative calm prevailed throughout the service, according to Miss Turner. "It seemed as if the animals knew where they were. There was a kind of quiet. Even the big Shepherds were calm," she said.

The message behind the "Blessing of the Animals" service is in keeping with the ongoing work of the Meriden Humane Society. "We have a moral obligation to animals," Miss Turner said. "It's not something we can abuse or neglect.

"I just hope Dr. Hanchey was happy enough with the service to consider doing it on a regular basis each year. I would like to see this service expanded to involve all the churches, and to hold the ceremony at Hubbard Park," the president said.

Blessed animals

Pets of almost every sort were blessed at St. Andrew's Church Sunday during a special afternoon service led by the Rev. Dr. Howard Hanchey. The minister, amid the barks and howls, kept his sermon brief, noting that "the Creation must have been noisy too."

DAYS OF ROGATION, TAKING CARE OF GOD'S WORLD

Ascension day follows Easter by forty days. The Sunday before Ascension day is generally known as "Rogation Sunday," in the Anglican tradition, and the three days following it as the "days of rogation."

These few days offer Christian education a perfect gift for our time. The word "rogation" comes from the Latin *rogare*, meaning "to ask for" or "to pray." Rogation Sunday was a day set aside for special prayers on behalf of the coming season's crops.

Little is done about Rogation Sunday today, but in early rural England, when the inhabitants' dependence on the produce of the land was greater than it is now, every parish made a big thing not only of Sunday but of the next three days.

On the Monday, Tuesday, and Wednesday preceding Ascension day, residents of the parish filed through their community, breaking frequently for prayers, sermons, and picnics. It was serious and reverent worship, but the worshipers managed also to have a good deal of fun along the way.

Ancient rogation can help us today. Our forests are dying from environmental pollutants; in the Midwest, groundwater is in short supply; streams and rivers are no longer pure; and ask any hunter about what is happening to the birds and the other animals.

The rogation days can serve us well. Use them to focus attention on how we obtain our food, but even more important, to detail a vision of good care for the world.

You cannot make an impact on global issues, but teaching and learning can become experiential when you point out the ways in which we can take care of our church grounds, our yards at home, and the woods and fields around us.

Some may want to plant something around the church, or to transplant seeds previously grown in the classroom. Throughout the summer, as the plants flower you will be reminded that at least a part of our Christian heritage encourages a tender response to our environment.

DAY OF THE ASCENSION

The commemoration of Jesus' ascension takes places on the fortieth day after Easter. It always falls on a Thursday. A pity, because it is all too easily missed.

I am not going to get into *how* Jesus left us; the plain fact is, he *did*. Ascension is the "official" day to remove the Christ Candle from its place in the nave of the church. With great fanfare it is removed on the first Sunday after the Ascension. A great procession is one way to ceremonialize it, and then we must wait until next year's advent to experience "light" in this way again.

For children, this event especially encourages an expectant attitude. And so we turn next to Pentecost.

PENTECOST

On the Sunday following, parish worship celebrates—with balloons and banners, grand parades, maybe a skit or play, lots of song—the gift of God's spirit. The day is called Pentecost, from the Greek *pente*, and falls fifty days after Easter.

Pentecost may also be the day of church-school graduation, if Easter has not occurred too early, and it is a grand time to receive preregistrations for next year's work, too.

Members of the Sunday school can be presented to the parish at large, certificates of participation given, and the year's formal learning concluded. Parties will probably be scheduled by many classes, and, at some point in the morning's festivities, a large reception for the entire parish is appropriate.

Endings like these, celebrated with everyone in mind, are also a grand advertisement with which to attract next year's teachers. Details like these separate lively Christian education from those programs that simply limp along.

MOTHER'S DAY AND FATHER'S DAY

Mother's Day falls in May and Father's Day in June. Though Mother's Day has its historical roots in the Middle Ages, neither it nor its counterpart is a church festival. Both days, however, like Paul's altar to an "unknown god" (Acts 17:23), potentially can communicate something of who God is and the human needs for which he provides.

Mother's Day is rooted in the early medieval Church. It took place not on a warm May Sunday but on a damp, chilly Sunday in March. It was known in England as "Mothering Sunday."

Here is how it got its name: The epistle designated for the fourth

Sunday in Lent was a part of Paul's letter to the Galatians. In it Paul spoke of "Jerusalem . . . which is our mother . . ." (Galatians 4:26). He was trying to persuade a small, new Church in Asia Minor to support the work of the mother Church in Jerusalem, which had fallen on hard times.

This Sunday in Lent was the time the English Church, centuries later, remembered mother Jerusalem, too. In those days, most boys and girls lived away from home, learning trades as apprentices to masters or serving as maids. From a twentieth-century perspective, they had a harsh life. On the mid-Lent Sunday when this lesson was read, the children were given permission to return home and visit their "mother church"—the home parish where they had been baptized as infants. It was also a day of family reunion.

The children carried gifts to their parents, and placed them about the church altar. A typical gift for mother was a simnel cake, a rich kind of plum or fruit cake made of simnel, or "fine" flour—the best that could be bought. Of course, tradition permitted the Lenten fast to be broken on this one day of the season.[4]

Our modern Mother's- and Father's-Day traditions spring from this event, and both Sundays are opportunities to celebrate family life and the importance of parents. Mother's Day can also remind us that God is far more than male and female images.

I am aware of how often books (this manual included) and journals refer to God in the masculine. The biblical tradition justifying this stance is very old but acknowledgment of the feminine in the Godhead is just as ancient. Scripture provides numerous illustrations, and even late in the last century the Reverend Basil Wilberforce, Archdeacon of Westminster, preached at Westminster Abbey a thoughtful sermon entitled *The Motherhood of God*.[5]

Christian education demands that we identify God's presence in the world as clearly and precisely as is humanly possible. Our children deserve sensitive teachers who are alive to the richness of God's spirit as it, through Scripture's witness, brings us increasingly near God's throne of Grace.[6]

GATHERING LOOSE ENDS

It is not too late to ask your clergy to explain how visits to the sick are made. Perhaps you could join them on a Sunday afternoon visit to the hospital, maybe bringing flowers from the altar. Plans must be made beforehand, but hospital workers are more than glad to help with the care of their patients.

Bedside communion is a lovely event, and the use of aromatic oil in the anointing of the sick makes for good teaching. How else, one wonders, can we encourage each successive generation's appreciation of care unless we teach about it?

You will probably be planning a final visit to the shut-in you adopted, and now is a grand time to share again some of what you studied this year.

By now you have become part of your pupils' world, and they a part of yours. To remember the good times just past, try brainstorming. It is easily done by seating your students in a circle and then, by snapping your fingers rhythmically, establishing a cadence so that your students can chime in, one after another, with whatever first pops into their minds. Have a colleague write these spontaneous thoughts out on a piece of paper, and you will see a clear picture emerge of what your students' "life" was like during the last nine months.

Goodbyes are important, and a year's end ought not to pass without acknowledgment.

SOME SUNDAY TEACHING POSSIBILITIES

In some years this term may be as long as ten weeks, in others as brief as five or six weeks. It all depends on when Easter Sunday falls and on when you choose to end the church-school year for summer vacation. But classroom possibilities are numerous.

FIRST SUNDAY:

—This is called "Low Sunday," mainly because attendance is usually way down.
—Relax and have fun.
—How about taking time with your class to plan the term's activity?
—Explore the appearances of Jesus after the resurrection.
—The Christ Candle has been lighted again.
—Think about dramatizing some of Jesus' activity.
—Can you use the choir and the organist?
—Make plans now to gather plants for Rogation Sunday.
—Can parents participate with your pupils in the planting?

—During Lent did you plant things that can be moved outside, beautifying the church building for the summer?

SECOND SUNDAY:

—Continue studying Jesus' appearances.
—Develop ways to encourage your class to wonder how people felt when they saw Jesus.
—How about Thomas touching Jesus' wounds?
—Things are winding down; relax.
—Begin to say goodbye.
—Sometime in May mention the blessing of the animals.
—What animals will your children bring?
—Plan on what plants you will plant on Rogation Sunday.
—Will you just plant seeds?
—Study St. Paul's conversion after he saw Jesus.
—Wonder what it was like on the road to Damascus.
—Think about dramatizing some of Jesus' deeds.
—Could you present the play to the adult class?

THIRD SUNDAY:

—Mention the blessing of the animals.
—Use St. Paul's story.
—Have you ever read Taylor Caldwell's *Great Lion of God,* a story about St. Paul? It is very good.

FOURTH SUNDAY:

—Look at the ways Jesus brought life to the persons with whom he lived.
—Look at some of the stories he used to teach about life.
—"Good Shepherd" Sunday is always the fourth Sunday of Easter. Check the readings and collect to see why.
—St. Paul heard the same stories about Jesus that you are using.
—What about drama?
—Use the choir and the organist.
—Another great book for you is Caldwell's *Dear and Glorious Physician,* the story of St. Luke.
—Bake bread and present it in the Eucharist.
—How about each class making a special banner about Jesus helping people? We will display them on graduation day.

FIFTH SUNDAY (or the Sunday Before Ascension):

—Rogation Sunday.
—Plant outside.
—Take a walk and notice life being born on the trees.
—Sunday after next the Christ Candle will leave us.
—Who comes in its place?
—For the graduation exercises make a special banner about St. Paul.
—Would you like to have someone come to class and tell the history of your church, and the life God has brought the community through it?

ASCENSION DAY.

SIXTH SUNDAY:

—The Christ Candle will leave us.
—We will have a great procession of the candle out of the church.
—We will prepare for Pentecost and graduation on next Sunday.
—Have you said goodbyes?
—What about the stories of Jesus that St. Paul heard—are you using them?
—Making banners is a good way to learn some of the stories.
—What about a final visit to your shut-in?
—Fill in the graduation certificates.
—How are the banners coming along?

PENTECOST:

—We celebrate the coming of God's Holy Spirit.
—Fill in the graduation certificates.
—Prepare for graduation.
—Encourage your students to attend.
—Have you said goodbyes?
—You can invite the parents to attend the last class sessions.
—Perhaps they would like to help with the banners.

EIGHTH SUNDAY:

—The First Sunday of Pentecost/church-school graduation.
—Presentation of the graduation certificates.
—A great procession of classes, with banners, balloons, and flowers.
—A big party in the parish hall for the whole parish community follows.

Notes

1. "God's creatures blessed at St. Andrew's service." *The Morning Record and Journal* (Meriden, CT), 31 May 1977.
2. Photo Credit, *New Haven Register* (New Haven, CT), 15 May 1978.
3. *The Hymnal of the Protestant Episcopal Church, 1940* (New York: The Church Pension Fund, 1940), Hymns 311, 346, 313, 276.
4. Adapted from *The Watchman* (Piedmont Parish, Delaplane, VA), 7 March 1983.
5. Basil Wilberforce, D.D., *Sanctification by the Truth: Sermons Preached For the Most Part in Westminster Abbey* (New York: E. P. Dutton & Co.), 40.
6. Thomas C. Oden, *Pastoral Theology, Essentials in Ministry* (Cambridge: Harper and Row, 1983). Oden briefly develops, on pages 6 to 7, an inclusive vision of ministry and, in chapter 4, illuminates from Scripture the leadership of women in the pastoral office. Church-school teachers will find his discussion concise and helpful and may want to explore some of his examples in class. (See also endnote 2, Ch. 4.)

Appendix: Biblical Citations

CHAPTER 2

Romans 8:28—All things work together for good. . . . P. 12.

CHAPTER 4

Revelation 3:20—God seeks communion with us. P. 24.
Mark 16:5—The Great Commission. P. 25.
Ephesians 3:20—God is actively for us. P. 25.
Matthew 10:30, Luke 12:7—God knows the number of hairs on our heads. P. 26.
Deuteronomy 33:27—God's everlasting arms. P. 26.
Genesis 2:7—God's creative wind. P. 26.
Revelation 3:20—Faith is the human response to God's presence. P. 28.
Acts 17:16f—Paul introduces God to the people of Athens. P. 35.
Revelation 3:20—Conversion is often gradual. P. 35.
Matthew 23:37f, Luke 13:34f—Jesus describes himself as a mother hen. P. 40.

CHAPTER 5

Daniel 6:16f—Daniel cast to the lions. P. 41.
Luke 10:33f—The parable of the Good Samaritan. P. 43.
The Book of Ruth—On God's love. P. 43.
Exodus 1:8–15:22—The Hebrew exodus from Egypt. P. 47.
Acts 7—Stephen is stoned. P. 51.

John 14:2—The many mansions of God bring peace to some. P. 56.
Deuteronomy 33:27—God's everlasting arms. P. 56.

CHAPTER 6

Isaiah 6:1—God's call to Isaiah. P. 58.

CHAPTER 9

Genesis 12:1—God's promise to Abraham. P. 98.
Genesis 27f—Jacob's deception and God's care. P. 98.
Genesis 34—Joseph saves his family. P. 98.
Exodus 3:1—The Hebrews flee from Egypt. P. 98.
1 Samuel 16:1—David and Goliath. P. 98.
Ruth—Naomi, Ruth, and their love. P. 98.
Acts 9:1-30—The conversion of Paul. P. 98.

CHAPTER 10

Isaiah 42:5f—God's promise to create again. P. 115.
Genesis 1. P. 115.
Isaiah 45:4f—God promises a new light. P. 115.
Isaiah 60:1f—The glory of the light, the Lord. P. 115.
Psalm 119—God is like a lamp. P. 116.
Luke 1:26—The announcement to Mary of Jesus' birth. P. 120.
Luke 1:78—The light of Christ. P. 120.
Luke 1:39—Mary visits Elizabeth. P. 121.
Luke 1:13f—The birth of John the Baptist. P. 121.
Luke 2:1—Jesus' birth is near. P. 121.
Nehemiah 8:10—About Thanksgiving Day. P. 126.

CHAPTER 11

Matthew 17:2, Mark 9:2—The transfiguration of Jesus. P. 130.
Matthew 2:1—The slaughter of the children. P. 131.
Acts 6:8—The martyrdom of Stephen. P. 132.
Luke 2:21—The circumcision of Jesus. P. 132.
Luke 2:29—Simeon sings a song of thanksgiving. P. 132.
Genesis 37-Exodus 14—The Hebrew exodus from Egypt. P. 132.
Matthew 2:12f—God's deliverance and saving love. P. 132.
Exodus 11—The plagues on the Egyptians. P. 132.

Exodus 7:26—The Passover. P. 133.
Exodus 20—The Ten Commandments. P. 133.
Matthew 3:1f—Jesus is growing up. P. 133.
Matthew 3:13—Jesus is baptized by John. P. 133.
Matthew 25:21—Good news is hearing the words "Well done. . . ."
P. 134.
Mark 10:46—Bartimaeus gets his sight. P. 134.
Luke 5:18—A paraplegic walks. P. 134.
Luke 8:40f—Jarius' daughter lives again. P. 134.
Matthew 18:20—"When two or three are gathered in my name. . . ."
P. 135.
Jeremiah 1:4—"Before you were formed in the womb I knew you."
P. 137.
Exodus 13f—God's love as a pillar of fire and cloud. P. 137.
Acts 17:15f—Paul's trip to Athens. P. 139.

CHAPTER 12

Acts 5–8—Stephen's martyrdom. P. 150.
Luke 23:33f—Jesus' crucifixion. P. 151.
John 11:2f—Lazarus is raised by Jesus from the dead. P. 153.
1 Corinthians 15:35f—St. Paul uses a seed to describe death. P. 153.
Matthew 10:39—To find life we lose our life, to God. P. 153.
John 4:1—Jesus helps a Samaritan woman. P. 154.
John 9:1—A blind man receives his sight. P. 154.
John 8:2f—Jesus stops a stoning. P. 154.
Mark 11:15—Jesus overturns the tables in the Temple. P. 154.
Luke 7:11—Jesus restores the life of the widow's son. P. 154.
Mark 2:23—Jesus breaks the law. P. 154.
Jeremiah 12:1—"Why do the wicked prosper?" P. 157.
Psalm 46:1—"God is our refuge and strength. . . ." P. 159.
1 Kings 19:11—God's still small voice. P. 159.
Hebrews 2:9—God suffers with us. P. 161.
2 Corinthians 1:1f—We are not alone. P. 161.
Philippians 3:10—God is where we are. P. 161.
1 Kings 17—God raises the dead to life. P. 162.
John 11:28—Jesus raises Lazarus to life. P. 162.
Acts 9:3f—Saul watches Stephen stoned to death. P. 162.
Revelation 3:20—We open our lives to God's presence. P. 163.
Isaiah 11:1f—The stump of Jesse, Jesus' forbear. P. 164.

190   *Creative Christian Education*

1 Cor 15:35–43—A seed grows. P. 165.
Matthew 13:31, Mark 4:31, Luke 13:19—A mustard seed. P. 165.

CHAPTER 13

Acts 9f—Paul's conversion. P. 171.
Luke 24:13—Jesus meets his friends on the Emmaus Road. P. 172.
John 20:24—Thomas touches Jesus' wounds. P. 172.
Luke 24:41—Jesus eats fish with his friends. P. 172.
Luke 24:10f—Jesus' women friends are first to see an empty tomb.
   P. 172.
Mark 10:46—Bartimaeus gets his sight. P. 173.
Luke 17:11f—Ten lepers are healed. P. 173.
Luke 7:1f—Jesus heals a sick servant. P. 173.
Luke 10:29—The story of the Good Samaritan. P. 173.
Luke 15:11—The story of the Prodigal Son. P. 174.
Luke 16:19—The story of the beggar Lazarus. P. 174.
Acts 8—Paul's presence at Stephen's death. P. 174.
1 Corinthians 11:17—Paul advises the Church on communion pro-
   tocol. P. 175.
Acts 17:23—Paul's visit to Athens, the altar to an unknown god.
   P. 180.
Galatians 4:26—"Jerusalem . . . which is our mother," on Mother's
   Day. P. 181.